THIRD EDITION

Now Hear This!

High-Beginning Listening, Speaking & Pronunciation

BARBARA H. FOLEY

INSTITUTE FOR INTENSIVE ENGLISH
UNION COUNTY COLLEGE, NEW JERSEY

HEINLE
CENGAGE Learning™

Australia • Brazil • Japan • Korea • Mexico • Singapore • Spain • United Kingdom • United States

Now Hear This!: High-Beginning Listening, Speaking & Pronunciation
3rd Edition
Barbara H. Foley

Publisher: Sherrise Roehr

Acquisitions Editor: Tom Jefferies

Assistant Editor: Marissa Petrarca

Director, US Marketing: Jim McDonough

Marketing Manager: Caitlin Driscoll

Content Project Manager: John Sarantakis

Print Buyer: Betsy Donaghey

Composition: Pre-Press PMG

Cover Design: The Creative Source

Library of Congress Control Number: 2008939904

ISBN-13: 978-1-4240-0379-2

ISBN-10: 1-4240-0379-2

Heinle
20 Channel Center
Boston, MA 02210
USA

Cengage Learning is a leading provider of customized learning solutions with office locations around the globe, including Singapore, the United Kingdom, Australia, Mexico, Brazil, and Japan. Locate your local office at: **international.cengage.com/region**

Cengage Learning products are represented in Canada by Nelson Education, Ltd.

Visit Heinle online at **elt.heinle.com**
Visit our corporate website at **cengage.com**

Printed in the U.S.A.
2 3 4 5 6 7 8 9 10   13 12 11 10

ACKNOWLEDGMENTS

In the revised edition of *Now Hear This!*, I was working from a treasure chest. The original text has been used by thousands of students over the past twenty years. By listening carefully, I have been able to apply student and teacher feedback plus new research in the ESL field to add, delete, and change features of the existing program. With much appreciation to the individuals below, the revised edition of *Now Hear This!* is hopefully up-to-date, effective, and enjoyable to use.

Thank you to my colleagues at Union County College. You've always been available to share ideas, test materials, and speak into a tape recorder. Special thanks to Howard Pomann, Dorothy Burak, Marinna Kolaitis, Liz Neblett, Larry Wollman, John McDermott, Litza Georgiou, and Andre DeSandies. A special thanks to David Papier for his input.

When writing, an author owes a special debt to researchers and theoreticians in the ESL field. Over the past several years, I have read journal articles and books on listening and strategies by the following individuals. Additionally, I was privileged to hear all of them speak at International TESOL conferences: Patricia Dunkel, Stephen Krashen, David Nunan, Joan Morley, Pat Wilcox Peterson, Jack Richards, David Menhelsohn, Rebecca Oxford, and Penny Ur.

Finally, thank you, Bill, for your constant support and confidence in me.

CONTENTS

TO THE TEACHER

English as a Second Language learners are surrounded by sounds—conversations, announcements, music, television, radio, instructions. Listening is often their primary source of language input. Our challenge as teachers is to help students make sense of this incoming stream of language. As learners, our students need practice and listening strategies. As individuals, they need confidence in their ability to understand their new language.

Now Hear This! 3rd edition is a listening, pronunciation, and speaking text for high-beginning and low-intermediate students of ESL. It develops listening skills using high-interest narratives and informal conversations. The text and accompanying audio program may be used with college-level students, adult programs, and high school classes. The materials are both easy to use and highly effective in a language laboratory.

Now Hear This! is the second of two titles designed to develop aural/oral communication skills for high-beginning and low-intermediate students. *Listen to Me!* meets the needs of students at the beginning to high-beginning levels.

Teachers who are familiar with the second edition of *Now Hear This!* will be familiar with the thematic, easy-to-use format of the text. But, a look at the table of contents will reveal that the text has been thoroughly updated. There are seven new units, with titles such as *Cell Phones, Credit Cards, Starting Your Own Business,* and *Carjackings.* Two other units, *The Changing Face of the United States* and *Jobs for the Future* have been updated with current information and census statistics.

The text now boasts three new features. As an introduction to the topic, *Person on the Street* presents the short responses of several college students and adults on the topic of the unit. These were recorded and transcribed, then rerecorded in the audio studio, with the fillers and hesitations present in the original audio.

Each unit includes a short note-taking activity. Students are introduced to a variety of note-taking formats, such as writing numbers, completing check lists, recording reasons or details, or writing the steps in a process.

Finally, there is an emphasis in the book on learning strategies. Sample strategies include predicting what information might be heard, using visual cues to aid in understanding, listening for tone of voice, and listening for main idea and details. For many students, a two or three minute listening can seem overwhelming, a sea of words washing over them. Listening strategies offer suggestions to students on how to focus their listening and how to become more effective listeners. Classroom discussion of listening strategies can help students develop techniques for comprehension. In addition, individual students can describe the strategies they use, offering further suggestions. For many students, it is reassuring to learn from other students that listening comprehension takes time and practice and that their understanding will improve gradually.

UNIT ORGANIZATION

Each of the fourteen thematic units in *Now Hear This!* includes eight sections. They are designed to introduce the context of the main listening and present the main listening and related conversations. Two sections focus on individual grammar and pronunciation features in the unit. Finally, students are given an opportunity to sit in groups and discuss the content of the listening.

Before You Listen

A photo or illustration introduces the theme of the unit and draws the students into the topic. It relates the topic to students' own lives; for example, by asking them to identify the state and area in which they live on the census map or by checking the features that are important to them in a job. The activity may also draw on the students' background information by asking what facts they may know about diabetes, credit cards, famous events, or other topics. Teachers should encourage students to comment on the person and/or activities in the picture. Students may ask for a few vocabulary words shown in the picture. At times, there are questions or a short paragraph related to the illustration.

Listening 1: Person on the Street

Dozens of college students and adults were asked questions about the topics in this text. *What do you do? Do you like your job? Was anyone at your work ever fired? What for? How long do you talk on your cell phone every day? Who do you talk to?* For each unit, three to five responses were chosen and recorded. These short listenings further introduce the topic and provide vocabulary and ideas which students may hear in the main listening. After listening to the responses, students complete a short activity related to the content.

Vocabulary

The *Vocabulary* section defines several words from the listening passage. Students then complete sentences with the correct word. At times, there is an additional vocabulary activity that encourages students to apply the new vocabulary they have learned.

Listening 2: Narrative or Dialogue

The unit presents a recorded story or dialogue, focusing on the theme. The stories are approximately two to four minutes in length. Before students listen, a listening strategy is presented. It is helpful to further discuss the strategy with the class. Then, as the students listen, they try to apply the strategy to the audio. There are several activities within this section, all designed to gradually increase the students' understanding of the content. They may be asked to identify ideas that a speaker mentions, indicate on a map whether the population of certain cities has increased or decreased, check the outlook for specific jobs, take short notes, put events in order, etc.

Depending on the level of the students, the teacher may play the audio in its entirety. Then, it may be helpful to play the audio in sections, a few sentences at a time. In one activity in each unit, students are asked to tell the class any information they remember about the story. The focus here is not on structure, but on the comprehension of the story. One student may only be able to recall one small piece of information. Another may be able to remember many facts. Students who may have had difficulty understanding the selection will learn from their classmates.

Structure

In the first part of each unit, the emphasis is on content. In the next two sections, the emphasis shifts to listening discrimination. In the first exercise in Structure, students focus on verb tense. Although there is a variety of tenses within each selection, one tense often predominates. Students complete sentences from the listening passage with the correct verb. This is followed by a dictation of five or six sentences from the audio.

Pronunciation

Within each listening selection, a recurring pronunciation feature has been highlighted; for example, *can* vs. *can't, and* vs. *or,* the reduction of *h* in *his/him/her,* linking, or stressed syllables. A pronunciation box with a short explanation and one or more examples presents the feature. Students circle the phonological item they hear, complete sentences with the correct word, or mark stress or intonation. Then, students sit with a partner and practice saying the sentences that were presented.

Listening 3: Conversations

This section begins with three to six short conversations or interview comments related to the topic. The interviews are transcriptions of authentic language. The conversations were role-played and scripted, with liberal use of expressions and replies that were recorded while gathering natural speech for this text. The conversations are purposely pitched at a more difficult level than the narratives, so that students begin to realize that they do not need to understand every word in a conversation.

In the exercises that follow, students focus on general meaning and important details. Further exercises develop listening strategies, helping students to become familiar with common conversation techniques, such as checking or repeating information, asking for a further explanation, or deciding on sentence intonation.

Speaking

The unit ends with a *Speaking* section that allows students to share personal information, ideas and opinions. Students sit in small groups of three or four students so that every student has an opportunity to participate. The topics are open-ended and stimulate discussion. For example, the groups have to decide what a person should do in an emergency situation, explain a recent dream, talk about the job outlook for various jobs, discuss cell phone plans, decipher text messages, or make up a story or dialogue about a series of pictures. Several units offer suggestions for follow-up activities on the Internet, directing students to share the information they have obtained with their classmates.

Now Hear This! is a complete and fully-integrated program for students and teachers alike. Complementing the student text is an audio program containing all of the listening passages and follow-up activities.

DO YOU LIKE YOUR JOB?

BEFORE YOU LISTEN

A Job Features   You are looking for a job. What do you think are the five most important features of a job? Check five statements.

_____ 1. The salary is good.

_____ 2. The job has medical benefits.

_____ 3. The job is near my home.

_____ 4. The boss is helpful.

_____ 5. The coworkers are friendly.

_____ 6. There is some future in this job.

_____ 7. The hours are good.

_____ 8. I can learn a new skill or get some training in this job.

_____ 9. I can sit at a desk.

_____ 10. The work is interesting.

B Discuss   Look at the jobs above. Which job would you like? Give your reasons.

LISTENING 1: PERSON ON THE STREET

Interview questions:

- *What do you do?*
- *Do you like your job?*
- *What do you like about your job?*

Ⓐ Listen for Information Listen to each person talk about his/her job. Complete the information. Write two things that each person likes about his or her job.

CD 1; Track 1

Speaker 1 is a _____.

The job is _____. This person also likes _____.

Speaker 2 is a _____.

This person likes _____ and _____.

Speaker 3 is _____.

This person likes _____ and _____.

Listening Note: Taking time to think

When speaking, people often take time to think about their response or answer. They sometimes repeat the question they hear or use expressions like:

Let me think . . .

Let's see . . .

Hmmm . . .

Ⓑ Taking Time to Think Listen to each worker again and match the conversation with the expression(s) each person uses.

CD 1; Track 1

____ CONVERSATION 1	a. Let me think . . . .
____ CONVERSATION 2	b. Hmm . . . What do I like?
____ CONVERSATION 3	c. Let's see . . . Well,

VOCABULARY

A Key Words   Discuss the new vocabulary. Then, complete the sentences below.

to recognize	to be able to identify; to see that something is familiar
overtime	extra hours of work, usually paid at a higher hourly rate
token	a round piece of metal that looks like a coin, often deposited in a machine to pay for using a road, bridge, or bus
lucky	having good fortune or good things happen
over and over	again and again
fumes	smoke or gas, usually from a car
to complain	to say that you are unhappy or not satisfied with something
promotion	a better position at work
salary	the money a person receives each week or month for their job

1. There are not many jobs in this area. She was _____ to find a job.

2. I can _____ any car and tell you what year it is.

3. My friend received a _____; she's now the manager.

4. Gas _____ are one cause of pollution.

5. My boss _____ if we take one extra minute at break time.

6. My _____ is $500 a week.

7. My work is boring. I do the same thing _____.

8. Last week, I worked five hours _____.

9. The toll is fifty cents. If you use a _____, it's only forty cents.

LISTENING 2: DO YOU LIKE YOUR JOB?

 Listening Note: Guessing

When you know the topic that the person is going to speak about, it is often possible to guess, or predict, the information you might hear in the talk. As you listen, you can compare your ideas to those of the speaker.

Ⓐ Guess You are going to hear two toll collectors talk about their jobs. Before you listen, try to guess some of the information you might hear.

1. What are some of this person's job responsibilities?

   _____

2. What do you think this person likes about the job?

   _____

3. What do you think this person doesn't like about the job?

   _____

CD 1; Track 2

B Listen for Information   Listen as two toll collectors talk about their jobs. Who likes the job? Who doesn't like the job? After you listen, tell the class any other information you remember about the story.

CD 1; Track 2

C Listen and Check   Listen to each speaker again. Check the job features that each person talks about.

Job Feature	Woman	Man
1. the hours	_____	_____
2. the weather	_____	_____
3. the boss	_____	_____
4. overtime	_____	_____
5. the salary	_____	_____
6. the coworkers	_____	_____
7. the benefits	_____	_____
8. a promotion	_____	_____

Listening Note: Understanding tone of voice

A person's tone of voice can show his/her opinion or feelings. For example, tone of voice can show if the person feels angry, excited, bored, happy, or sad.

CD 1; Track 3

D Tone of Voice   You will hear ten sentences about work. Listen to each person's tone of voice to help you decide if the speaker is describing something he likes or doesn't like about the job.

1. likes   doesn't like
2. likes   doesn't like
3. likes   doesn't like
4. likes   doesn't like
5. likes   doesn't like
6. likes   doesn't like
7. likes   doesn't like
8. likes   doesn't like
9. likes   doesn't like
10. likes   doesn't like

STRUCTURE

> ▶ **Grammar Note: Simple Present Tense**
>
> The third person (*he, she, it*) ends with an *s* in the simple present tense.
>
> | | |
> |---|---|
> | I like | We like |
> | You like | You like |
> | He like**s** | They like |

Ⓐ Simple Present Tense Complete the sentences with the verb in the present tense.

give	want	take	ask	recognize
have	complain	collect	buy	hate

1. I really ___**hate**___ this job. It's time to look for a new one.

2. I _____ fifty cents.

3. The smell of gas _____ me a headache.

4. My boss _____ about my work.

5. I don't _____ to collect tolls for the rest of my life.

6. I _____ tolls from drivers.

7. Many drivers _____ tokens.

8. Sometimes a driver _____ for directions.

9. I _____ every make and model of car.

10. I _____ medical benefits.

Ⓑ Dictation Listen and write the sentences you hear.

CD 1; Track 4

1. _____

2. _____

3. _____

4. _____

5. _____

PRONUNCIATION

CD 1; Track 5

Pronunciation Note: And, Or

And often sounds like *ąnd*. *Or* often sounds like *ər*.

My hands and feet are cold.

I can't see my family or friends.

CD 1; Track 5

A And / Or Listen carefully and complete the sentences with *and* or *or*.

1. I sit _____ **or** _____ stand.

2. I usually work on Saturday _____ Sunday.

3. I can recognize every make _____ model.

4. I have medical benefits for myself _____ my family.

5. It's the same thing over _____ over.

6. I work eight _____ nine hours a night.

7. In the winter, the work is cold _____ boring.

8. I'm going to quit _____ find a new job.

B Partner Practice Sit with a partner. Say one of the sentences from each pair below. Your partner will point to the sentence you are saying.

1. a. I always work on Saturday and Sunday.
   b. I always work on Saturday or Sunday.

2. a. His car is blue and black.
   b. His car is blue or black.

3. a. I'm going to travel to Spain and France.
   b. I'm going to travel to Spain or France.

4. a. My brother is going to visit in June and July.
   b. My brother is going to visit in June or July.

5. a. He bought a shirt and a sweater.
   b. He bought a shirt or a sweater.

6. a. You need a pen and a pencil.
   b. You need a pen or a pencil.

7. a. Please buy juice and milk.
   b. Please buy juice or milk.

LISTENING 3: GUESS THE JOB

> **Listening Note: Getting the main idea**
> You often will not understand every word in a conversation. If you can understand some of the words, you can get the main idea.

CD 1; Track 6

Ⓐ Getting the Main Idea You will hear each person talk about his or her job. As you listen, write two or three key words that give an idea of the person's job. Try to guess the job.

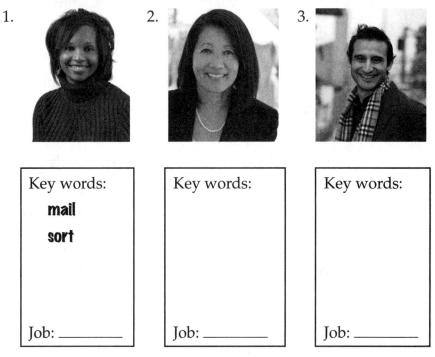

1.

Key words:

mail

sort

Job: _____

2.

Key words:

Job: _____

3.

Key words:

Job: _____

CD 1; Track 6

Ⓑ Match Read the statements below. Then, listen to each conversation again. Write the number of the correct photo next to each statement. Sit with a partner and check your answers.

____ 1. This person likes his coworkers.

____ 2. This person gets to work early.

____ 3. This person does not have medical benefits.

____ 4. This person works outside for part of the day.

____ 5. This person likes her boss.

SPEAKING

A Interview   Interview a classmate about his or her job. Take notes about the information. Then, join another pair of students and tell about your partner's job.

1. Where do you work?	
2. What do you do?	
3. What are your hours?	
4. What benefits do you have?	
5. Do you ever work over time?	
6. What do you like about your job?	
7. What don't you like about your job?	
8. How did you find this job?	
9. How long have you been working there?	

B Job Discussion   Discuss each job below. Would you like the job? Explain why or why not.

Front desk clerk. Claremeont Hotel. FT evening position. Exp. with computers. We will train.

Long distance and local truck driver for large furniture store. Valid and clean DL required. Must have exp. with furniture assembly.

Bank teller, FT. Exp. with handling money, good communication skills, and strong math skills. Computer skills a must.

C Complete Sit in a group of two or three students. Complete the paragraph about the cook in the picture below. Give several reasons for your opinion. When you are finished, share your story with the class.

My name is _____. I'm a cook at

_____ and I really hate / love this job.

_____

_____

_____

_____

_____

_____

HURRICANE!

Saffir-Simpson Hurricane Scale		
Category	Wind Speed	Damage
1	74–95 mph 119–153 km/hr	Minor damage Tree branches, some power lines come down
2	96–110 mph 154–177 km/hr	Moderate damage Some damage to signs, trees, windows and roofs Minor flooding
3	111–130 mph 178–209 km/hr	More serious damage to homes Many trees come down Some flooding
4	131–155 mph 210–249 km/hr	Serious damage to buildings Destroys windows and doors, many roofs come off Major flooding near the coast Need to evacuate areas near coast
5	155+ mph 250+ km/hr	Catastrophic damage Destroys many homes and buildings Heavy flooding Need to evacuate areas near coast

BEFORE YOU LISTEN

A **What Would You Take?** A hurricane is a strong tropical storm that brings high winds and heavy rain. In many parts of the world, a hurricane is called a typhoon or a cyclone. Radio and television give warning of a hurricane several days in advance. At times, thousands of people evacuate their homes and leave the area. If you had to evacuate your home, what are six items that you would take with you?

1. _____ 4. _____

2. _____ 5. _____

3. _____ 6. _____

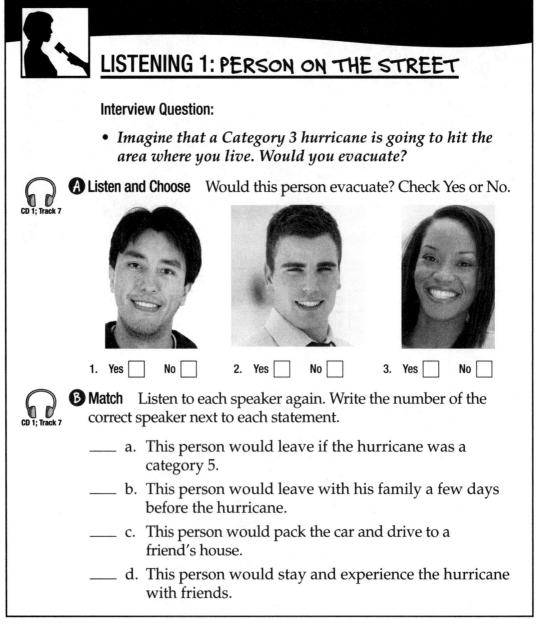

LISTENING 1: PERSON ON THE STREET

Interview Question:

- *Imagine that a Category 3 hurricane is going to hit the area where you live. Would you evacuate?*

CD 1; Track 7

A **Listen and Choose** Would this person evacuate? Check Yes or No.

1. Yes ☐ No ☐   2. Yes ☐ No ☐   3. Yes ☐ No ☐

CD 1; Track 7

B **Match** Listen to each speaker again. Write the number of the correct speaker next to each statement.

____ a. This person would leave if the hurricane was a category 5.

____ b. This person would leave with his family a few days before the hurricane.

____ c. This person would pack the car and drive to a friend's house.

____ d. This person would stay and experience the hurricane with friends.

VOCABULARY

A Key Words Discuss the new vocabulary. Then, complete the sentences.

category	group
coast	the land near the ocean
to fill up	to fill the gasoline tank of a car or truck
to grow	to become larger
to issue	to give or send information
plywood	a kind of wood that is used to build houses
wind	the movement of the air outdoors
to not take a chance	to stay safe; to keep away from danger

1. The hurricane *was* a Category 1, but it's _____ stronger and it's now a Category 2.

2. A _____ 5 hurricane is the strongest and most dangerous.

3. The gas is almost on *Empty*. We need _____ at the next gas station.

4. The governor _____ an order to evacuate because of the hurricane.

5. I like living near the _____ because I can go swimming in the summer.

6. In a Category 5 hurricane, the _____ can be over 150 miles per hour (249 km/hr).

7. Before a hurricane, many people put _____ over their windows.

8. I'm _____ going _____. I'm going to evacuate.

LISTENING 2: A NEWS REPORT

Listening Note: Using a picture to help in understanding

Before you listen, look at the picture, photo, or other artwork. It will help you understand what you hear. Ask yourself questions, for example: Who is talking? What are they talking about? Where are they? What are the people doing?

A Using a Picture Answer the questions about the picture.

1. What time of the year is it?

2. What is the weather?

3. Where are these people?

4. Why is the girl putting the garbage can in the garage?

5. What is the boy putting in the car?

6. Why do you think the reporter is talking to this man?

7. What questions do you think the reporter is asking?

CD 1; Track 8

B Listen and Check A news reporter is talking with a man who is evacuating his home. Read the list: *Preparing to Evacuate.* Listen and check the things that this family is doing. Then, tell the class any other information you remember about this family's preparations for the hurricane.

Preparing to Evacuate

___ 1. Choose a place to go.

___ 2. Prepare your yard. Put everything inside.

___ 3. Put plywood on your windows.

___ 4. Fill your car with gas.

___ 5. Bring your medications.

___ 6. Get extra cash from the bank.

___ 7. Bring important documents.

___ 8. Turn off the gas, electricity, and water.

___ 9. Unplug your appliances.

Listening Note: Repeating information
After listening, review the information you heard. Try to repeat some of the sentences or ideas out loud or to yourself.

CD 1; Track 8

C Repeating Information Listen to the news report again. Sit with a partner and write five things that this family is doing to prepare to evacuate. With your partner, practice repeating the sentences.

1. **They are filling the car with gas.** _____

2. _____

3. _____

4. _____

5. _____

At times, you listen for a specific fact or piece of information. As you listen, have in mind the information you need and the vocabulary you will probably hear.

CD 1; Track 8

D Listen for Details   Read the questions below so that you know what information to listen for. Then, listen to the news report again and circle the correct answer.

1. How strong is the hurricane?
   a. It's a Category 1.
   b. It's a Category 2.
   c. It's a Category 3.

2. How strong are the winds?
   a. They're 8 miles an hour.
   b. They're 48 miles an hour.
   c. They're 80 miles an hour.

3. How fast is the hurricane moving?
   a. It's moving 8 miles an hour.
   b. It's moving 48 miles an hour.
   c. It's moving 80 miles an hour.

4. When is the storm going to hit?
   a. It's going to hit today.
   b. It's going to hit tomorrow.
   c. It's going to hit the day after tomorrow.

5. Where does Mr. Morales live?
   a. in Miami
   b. in Tampa
   c. in Orlando

6. Which statement is true?
   a. The governor gave the order to evacuate.
   b. A few people are evacuating, but most people are staying.
   c. Most people are evacuating, but a few people are staying.

7. How far is this family from the ocean?
   a. five miles
   b. eight miles
   c. seventy-five miles

8. How far is this family going to drive?
   a. two miles
   b. eight miles
   c. seventy-five miles

STRUCTURE

A Dictation   Listen and write the sentences you hear.

1. _____

2. _____

3. _____

4. _____

5. _____

6. _____

B Present Continuous Tense   Complete the sentences with the present continuous form of the verb.

put	move	take	grow
pick up	go	fill	watch

1. The storm **is moving** slowly.

2. It _____ stronger every hour.

3. Everyone _____ the weather channel on TV.

4. The Morales' family _____ to a relative's house.

5. They _____ the dog with them.

6. Mr. Morales _____ things in the garage.

7. Mrs. Morales _____ the car with gas.

8. She is also _____ a prescription at the drugstore.

PRONUNCIATION

Pronunciation Note: want to, need to, have to, has to, going to

When people speak, they often reduce the sound of *to* after these verbs. You don't hear the *t.*

going to – *gonna*	We aren't *gonna* stay.
want to – *wanna*	I *wanna* leave early.
need to – *needa*	We *needa* clean up the yard.
has to – *hasta*	She *hasta* get some gas.
have to – *haveta*	You don't *haveta* evacuate.

Note: When writing, always write *to*: need *to*

Ⓐ Listen and Complete Listen to each sentence and complete with the verb you hear.

1. I _____**want**_____ _____**to**_____ leave early.

2. We're _____ _____ leave soon.

3. She _____ _____ pick up the medication.

4. The hurricane is _____ _____ hit Florida.

5. We don't _____ _____ evacuate.

6. We _____ _____ clean up the yard.

7. We _____ _____ go before the roads are crazy.

8. My wife _____ _____ stop at the drugstore.

9. We _____ _____ get some extra cash.

10. We are _____ _____ take two cars.

Ⓑ Partner Practice Sit with a partner. Take turns saying each sentence in Exercise A. Try to reduce the sound of *to*.

LISTENING 3: A RADIO BULLETIN

A Listen and Complete Listen to the two hurricane warnings.
Complete the missing information. You can listen several times.

> A hurricane **watch** means that a hurricane is *possible* in an area
> within the next 36 hours.
>
> A hurricane **warning** means that a hurricane is *expected* in an area
> within the next 24 hours.

1. **Hurricane Watch:**

   The National Weather Service has issued a hurricane
   _____ for _____ Florida, along the Gulf
   Coast. Hurricane Ann is _____ miles west of Florida, moving at _____ miles an hour. It is a category
   _____ hurricane. Residents are urged to prepare
   for the storm, _____ their yards, and buy extra
   _____ and _____. It is important to have a
   _____ operated radio.

2. **Hurricane Warning:**

   The National Weather Service has issued a hurricane
   _____ for _____ Florida, along the Gulf
   Coast. Hurricane Ann is growing stronger and is now a
   category _____ hurricane. It is _____ miles
   from Sarasota, moving at _____ miles per hour. It
   will hit the coast tonight, about _____. The governor
   has issued an evacuation order for Sarasota county. All
   residents of Sarasota county who live within _____
   miles of the coast must prepare to _____ their
   homes immediately. All schools and businesses in Sarasota
   will be _____ tomorrow.

SPEAKING

Ⓐ Write a List There is a hurricane warning, but your family has decided not to evacuate your home. List five more things that you are doing to prepare for the hurricane.

1. **We are buying a flashlight and batteries.**

2. _____

3. _____

4. _____

5. _____

6. _____

Ⓑ Identify the Picture Write the name of the natural disaster under each picture.

snowstorm	tornado	volcano
earthquake	fire	flood

a. _____ b. _____ c. _____

d. _____ e. _____ f. _____

C Discuss Look at the natural disasters from Exercise B. Discuss the questions about each of these disasters.

1. Describe each disaster. What happens in each kind of disaster?

2. In which part of the world does each disaster occur?

3. Which of these natural disasters occur in your country?

4. Talk about a recent natural disaster in your country. Where and when did it occur? What was the loss of life, homes, and roads?

5. For a hurricane, people receive warning several days in advance. How much warning is there for these disasters?

6. How can people prepare for these disasters?

D Radio Bulletins Sit in a small group of two or three students. Choose a natural disaster from Exercise B. Prepare a radio bulletin, warning the listeners of a natural disaster. Explain when and where the disaster will hit. Tell people what to do. Share the bulletins with the class.

E Word Web When learning new words, a word web can be helpful. Place a word in the middle circle; then, write other words that you associate with the main word. Write four words that you associate with *hurricane*. Then, choose another natural disaster from the Unit and create a new Word Web. Compare your Word Webs with a partner.

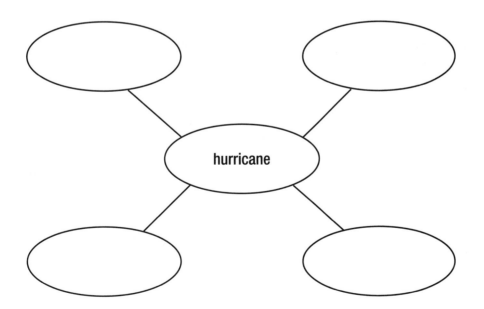

INTERNET ACTIVITIES

(A) Search for Information   Use the Internet. Check the weather for the next few days. Write two sites that you checked. Did they give the same forecast? Take notes on the lines below and compare the two forecasts.

_____

_____

_____

_____

_____

(B) Listen and Share   During the school year, listen for information about serious weather events throughout the world. In case of a major natural disaster, follow the news on the Internet. Share the information with your class.

DIABETES

BEFORE YOU LISTEN

 Discuss   Talk about diabetes and share any information you know.

THE POWER TO CONTROL
DIABETES
IS IN YOUR HANDS

National Diabetes Education Program

B Read   Read the article about diabetes. Underline and discuss any new vocabulary.

Diabetes

Diabetes is a disease in which the body does not make enough insulin or cannot use insulin the right way. Insulin helps the body use and control glucose. Glucose is blood sugar and it gives our bodies energy. When we eat, most of the food we eat turns into glucose. When we have diabetes, glucose stays in our bodies and builds up in the blood. Over time, this can cause serious health problems such as kidney disease, heart problems, and problems with the eyes.

There are two types of diabetes, Type 1 and Type 2. Type 1 diabetes often begins in childhood or the teenage years. The body makes little or no insulin. A person with Type 1 diabetes must take insulin to live. Type 2 diabetes usually begins when a person is an adult. In Type 2 diabetes, the body produces insulin, but it cannot use it correctly. More and more younger adults are developing Type 2 diabetes.

To determine if a person has diabetes, a doctor will give a glucose test. The most common diabetes test is the Fasting Plasma Glucose Test in which a person does not eat or drink for twelve hours. If the person's glucose level is between 100 and 125, it shows that the person has pre-diabetes. If the person's glucose level is over 126, it shows that the person has diabetes. Many people with diabetes use a small meter to check their glucose level. By working carefully with the doctor, eating correctly, exercising, and possibly taking medication, a person is often able to keep his or her glucose level close to normal.

C Complete   Complete the sentences with the information from the article.

1. In _____ the body does not make insulin.

2. _____ is blood sugar.

3. _____ helps the body use and control glucose.

4. In _____ the body does not use insulin correctly.

5. _____ is a common glucose test.

6. A person with a glucose level over _____ has diabetes.

7. People can check their glucose level with a _____.

8. One health problem caused by diabetes is _____.

LISTENING 1: PERSON ON THE STREET

Interview Question:

- *What do you know about diabetes?*

CD 1; Track 12

Ⓐ Listen for Key Words   Listen to each speaker. Circle the items that each person talks about.

Speaker 1

diet

insulin

blood sugar

meter

glucose

Speaker 3

diet

insulin

blood sugar

meter

glucose

Speaker 2

diet

insulin

blood sugar

meter

glucose

Speaker 4

diet

insulin

blood sugar

meter

glucose

Ⓑ Listen for Expressions   Listen to the four speakers again. Which words or expression does each person use to show he/she doesn't know a lot about the disease?

> ## Listening Note: Expressing Uncertainty about a Topic
>
> If a person only knows a little about a topic, she will usually tell you directly that she doesn't know the information or that she isn't sure about the information.

1. Speaker 1: **I know a little.** _____

2. Speaker 2: _____

3. Speaker 3: _____

4. Speaker 4: _____

VOCABULARY

Ⓐ Key Words   Discuss the new vocabulary. Then, complete the sentences below.

symptom	sign of a sickness, disease, or problem
disease	a sickness
to exercise	physical activity, such as walking or running
more likely	greater possibility
energy	the power to do work
glucose	natural sugar in the body
cure	make healthy by medication or treatment

1. He _____ at the gym five days a week.

2. One day doctors may find a _____ for cancer.

3. In the morning, I have a lot of _____, but in the evening I feel tired.

4. If you smoke, you are _____ to get lung cancer.

5. Chest pain is a _____ of a heart attack.

6. There is no cure for many _____.

7. _____ is a type of natural sugar in the body.

Ⓑ Apply the Vocabulary   Show your understanding of the new vocabulary by completing the information.

1. Name one exercise you enjoy.   _____

2. Name one symptom of a cold.   _____

3. Name one common disease.   _____

4. Name one disease that has no cure.   _____

5. Name one food that gives you energy.   _____

LISTENING 2: COULD YOU HAVE DIABETES?

> ## Listening Note: Understanding the main idea
>
> Short radio programs and other talks are often well organized into three or four different parts. Each part has a main idea.

A Listen for the Main Idea You are going to hear a short radio talk about diabetes: *Could you have diabetes?* This talk has three main ideas. Listen and number the ideas in the order you hear them.

CD 1; Track 13

_____ Symptoms of diabetes

_____ People who are more likely to get diabetes

_____ How to develop a health plan for diabetes

> ## Listening Note: Listening for *First, Second, Next, Finally*
>
> When speakers give a number of different ideas, instructions, or reasons, they use words like *First, Second, Next,* and *Finally.* These words show the listeners that they will hear a new idea.

B First, Second . . . Listen to the first part of the radio program again. You will hear six questions. Write the word that introduces each question.

CD 1; Track 13

1. _____, does someone in your family have diabetes?

2. _____, are you African-American, Hispanic, or Asian?

3. _____, do you know your blood pressure?

4. _____, are you heavy?

5. _____, how old are you?

6. _____, do you exercise?

C Using the Information Sit with a partner. Look at the information in Exercise B and put a check next to the three people who are more likely to get diabetes.

_____ 1. A person whose mother has diabetes.

_____ 2. A person who is Hispanic.

_____ 3. A person with low blood pressure.

_____ 4. A person who is thin.

_____ 5. A person who is over 60.

_____ 6. A person who exercises every day.

Listening Note: Taking Notes

When you take notes, do not write sentences. Only write the most important word or words to help you remember the idea.

CD 1; Track 13

D Note-Taking Listen to the second part of the radio program. Write five symptoms of a person with diabetes. Write only one word to help you remember each symptom. Then, listen to the health plan for people with diabetes. Take notes to help you remember the health plan. Write one or two words for each step.

Symptoms	Health Plan
1. _____	1. First, _____
2. _____	2. Second, _____
3. _____	3. Third, _____
4. _____	4. Next, _____
5. _____	5. Finally, _____

STRUCTURE

CD 1; Track 14

A Dictation Listen and write the sentences you hear.

1. _____

2. _____

3. _____

4. _____

5. _____

6. _____

B Short Questions Complete the *Yes/No* questions with *Is, Are, Do,* or *Does.*

1. _____ you African American, Hispanic, or Asian?

2. _____ you over 60?

3. _____ you have high blood pressure?

4. _____ you exercise?

5. _____ you overweight?

6. _____ someone in your family have diabetes?

7. _____ you thirsty?

8. _____ you heavy?

9. _____ you often feel tired?

10. _____ you gaining weight?

11. _____ you often hungry?

12. _____ you feel hungry all the time?

PRONUNCIATION

> ### Pronunciation Note: Syllables
> Words in English have one or more syllables. Listen to the vowels and the rhythm to help you hear the number of syllables.
>
> | One syllable | Two syllables | Three syllables | Four syllables |
> |---|---|---|---|
> | plan | doctor | exercise | medication |
> | check | today | important | especially |

A Syllables   Listen to these words. Write the number of syllables you hear.

1. sign __1__
2. Internet __3__
3. finally _____
4. symptoms _____
5. because _____

6. cure _____
7. problem _____
8. develop _____
9. diabetes _____
10. hungry _____

11. health _____
12. blood _____
13. necessary _____
14. diet _____
15. regular _____

> ### Pronunciation Note: Word Accent
> In each word of two or more syllables, one syllable is accented. We say that syllable longer and louder than the other syllable(s). We put an accent mark on that syllable.
>
> | Two syllables | Three syllables | Four syllables |
> |---|---|---|
> | dóctor | éxercise | medicátion |
> | todáy | impórtant | espécially |

B Word Accent   Listen to the words. Put an accent mark on the accented syllable.

1. peó ple
2. In ter net
3. fi nal ly
4. symp toms
5. be cause

6. in su lin
7. prob lem
8. de vel op
9. di a be tes
10. hun gry

11. me ter
12. care ful
13. nec es sar y
14. di et
15. reg u lar

C Partner Practice   Sit with a partner. Practice saying each word. Put the accent on the correct syllable.

LISTENING 3: AN INTERVIEW

CD 1; Track 17

A Listen for Information   You will hear an interview with a person with diabetes. Before you listen, read the questions that the interviewer asked. Then, listen and complete the information.

David, thank you for talking to me about this topic. I know you have diabetes and that you use a meter. Can you tell me more about the meter you use and what it shows?

1. David checks his blood sugar _____ times a day.

2. He takes a drop of blood from his _____, puts it on a special piece of _____ and puts it in the _____.

What is a normal blood sugar reading and what would a high reading be?

3. David checks his blood sugar in the _____ and after _____.

4. His reading should be between _____ and _____.

5. A reading below _____ is too low.

6. A reading above _____ is too high.

What are you supposed to do if your blood sugar is too high and what are you supposed to do if it is too low?

7. If David's blood sugar is too low, he _____.

8. If David's blood sugar is too high, he _____.

I know you are very careful of your diet. What can you eat and what can't you eat?

9. David eats lots of _____.

10. He can't eat _____.

11. The worst foods for David are _____ and _____.

David, any final thoughts?

12. According to David, most people have diabetes because _____.

13. Today, many children are developing diabetes because _____ and _____.

SPEAKING

A Discuss   Talk with a classmate about his or her health habits. Talk about your health. Is there anything you could do to have a healthier lifestyle?

1. Do you exercise three or more times a week?

2. Do you take vitamins?

3. Do you eat lots of fruit and vegetables?

4. Do you get seven or eight hours of sleep at night?

5. Do you know your blood pressure?

6. Do you drink six or more glasses of water every day?

7. Do you use sunscreen when you are in the sun?

8. Do you smoke?

9. Do you have any allergies?

10. What changes do you want to make in your lifestyle for better health?

B Health Problems   Work in a group. Write the names of three diseases or health problems. Write two symptoms of each.

Disease	Symptom	Symptom
_____	_____	_____
_____	_____	_____
_____	_____	_____

C Act It Out   Sit with a partner. Choose one of the health problems in Exercise B. Write a conversation between a doctor and a patient. You can use the questions below to help you. Two or three partners can act out their conversation for the class.

1. What's the problem?

   or What seems to be the problem?

2. How long have you been feeling like this?

3. Do you have a fever?

4. Do you have any chest pain?

5. What other symptoms do you have?

6. Does anyone in your family have _____?

   or Do you have a family history of _____?

7. Are you allergic to any kind of medication?

INTERNET ACTIVITY

Ⓐ Search for Information Choose one disease. Use the Internet to find information about the condition. Then, report back to your class about the information you found.

Disease: _____

Symptoms: _____

Cause: _____

Cure or Medication: _____

Two more facts: _____

_____

_____

Notes: _____

_____

_____

THE CHANGING FACE OF THE UNITED STATES

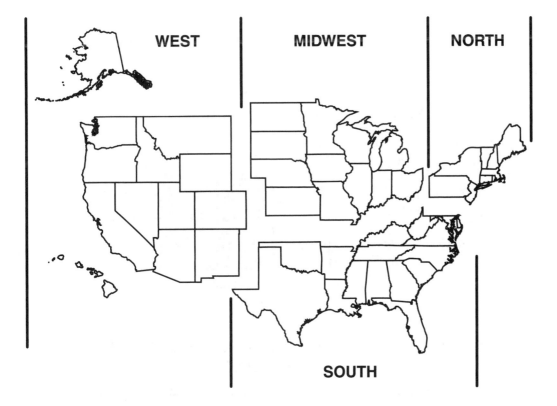

WEST   MIDWEST   NORTH

SOUTH

BEFORE YOU LISTEN

A Discuss the Map   Look at the map and answer the questions.

1. What state do you live in? Find it on the map.

2. What part of the country do you live in: North, South, Midwest, or West?

3. Do you have family or friends who live in other states? What states do they live in?

4. Are you thinking about moving to another area? If so, tell which area and give your reasons.

B Population Charts   The charts show the population of the United States in 2000 and the expected population in 2050. Look at the charts and answer the questions.

1. What was the population of the United States in 2000?

2. What percentage of the population was White? Black? Hispanic? Asian?

3. What will the population be in 2050?

4. What percentage of the population will be White? Black? Hispanic? Asian?

5. What are some of the biggest changes that will occur between 2000 and 2050?

Projected Population of the United States

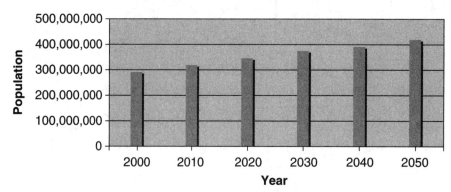

Population of the United States by Race and Hispanic Origin: 2000 to 2050

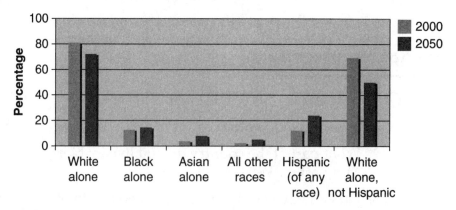

Source: U.S. Census Bureau, 2004, "U.S. Interim Projections by Age, Sex, Race, and Hispanic Origin,"

LISTENING 1: PERSON ON THE STREET

Interview Question:

- *These charts show the population of the United States in 2000 and the projected population in 2050. Are you surprised by any of the information?*

CD 1; Track 18

A Listen and Check Listen to each person talk about the chart information. Check the ethnic groups that each person speaks about.

	White	Hispanic	African-American	Asian
Speaker 1				
Speaker 2				
Speaker 3				
Speaker 4				

CD 1; Track 19

B Complete Listen and complete with the vocabulary about population.

1. The Hispanic population is _____.

2. And the African-American population is _____.

3. I thought the Asian population was _____.

4. The black population is _____.

5. The Hispanic population is going to _____ more than any other group.

6. The Hispanic population is _____.

7. I'm from California, and the population of Asians is much _____ there.

8. The number of Hispanics _____.

9. And here we have very _____ Asians.

C Write Write a word or expression from Exercise B that means the opposite.

go down - _____   lower - _____

change - _____   fall - _____

VOCABULARY

Ⓐ Match   A census collects information about the people who live in different cities and states. The census shows several types of households. Write the type of household under each picture.

> married couple with children   single man with children
>
> married couple with no children   single person
>
> single woman with children

_____

_____

_____

_____

_____

B Key Words   Discuss the new vocabulary. Then, complete
the sentences.

population	the number of people who live in an area
to grow	to become larger in size or number
life expectancy	the number of years that a person will probably live
new birth	a new child/baby
average	typical; ordinary
distance	the space between two places, e.g. the distance between New York and Washington
industry	company or business, usually one that makes a product
to retire	to stop work, usually at the age of 65
coast	land or area near the ocean

1. The _____ of the United States is over
   300 million people.

2. Every _____ adds to the population.

3. The population of Florida _____ because
   many people are moving there.

4. The _____ person in the United States
   graduates from high school.

5. The _____ from California to New York
   is 3,200 miles.

6. I am going _____ when I am 67.

7. Many new _____, like car manufacturers
   and computer companies, are moving to the South and West.

8. The _____ in the United States is
   77 years old.

9. We live near the _____, so we can swim
   in the ocean.

C Apply the Vocabulary   Answer the questions.

1. What country or state do you live in? What is the population?

2. What is the distance from your city to the capital?

3. Is your city near the coast? What is the distance from your
   city to the coast?

4. At what age do you plan to retire?

5. In your country or state, what industry is growing at
   this time?

LISTENING 2: THE CENSUS

Listening Note: Predicting

Before you listen, try to predict, or guess, some of the information you will hear. When you listen, you will listen more carefully to see if your guess is correct or not.

A Predict the Answer You are going to hear about how the population in the United States is changing. Before you listen, sit with a partner and try to guess the answers to these questions. After you listen, look at your answers again. Correct any answers that you need to change. What information in the talk surprised you?

1. How fast is the population of the United States growing?
   a. by 1 million people a year   b. by 4 million people a year

2. What percentage of the population of the United States was born in another country?
   a. 11%   b. 15%   c. 30%

3. What is the life expectancy for women?
   a. 75   b. 80   c. 100

4. What is the average age for men to marry?
   a. 22   b. 25   c. 27

5. What percentage of American homes have a married couple with children?
   a. 12%   b. 23%   c. 28%

6. What percentage of Americans live alone?
   a. 4%   b. 12%   c. 25%

7. How many people move each year?
   a. one in ten   b. one in seven   c. one in five

8. How far do most people move?
   a. a short distance   b. a long distance

9. Which of these states is growing the fastest?
   a. New York   b. Pennsylvania   c. Florida

10. Where are most new jobs?
    a. in the South and West   b. in the North and Midwest

B Listen and Complete Before you listen again, look at the statements below. Then, listen for the answers. Sit in a small group and compare your answers.

1. The United States takes a census every _____.

2. In 2050, the population will be over _____.

3. Most of the growth in population is from _____.

4. About _____% of new immigrants are from Mexico.

5. There are more women than men in the United States because _____.

6. The average age for women to marry is _____.

7. Many homes are a married couple with no children because _____.

8. Most people move in order to _____.

9. The North is growing slowly while the _____ and the _____ are growing fast.

10. _____ and _____ are both deciding to live in the warm, sunny South.

Listening Note: Introducing a new idea

When there are two or more reasons, causes, or other facts, listen for words like *First, Second, Next,* and *Finally.* They show that the speaker is going to start a new idea.

C Note-Taking Listen to the last part of the talk again. You are going to hear the three reasons that people are moving from the North and the Midwest to the South and the West. Use the words below to help you listen for the reasons.

1. The number one reason is _____.

2. The second reason is _____.

3. Finally, _____.

STRUCTURE

A Present Continuous Tense   Complete the paragraph with the verbs in the present continuous tense.

States like New York, Pennsylvania, and Massachusetts _____ (grow) slowly. States like Florida, Texas, and Nevada _____ (grow) very fast. The number one reason is jobs. Many large industries in the North _____ (close) or _____ (move) to the South or out of the country. Most new jobs are in the South or West. These areas need workers; they _____ (look) for teachers, builders, cooks, and store workers. The second reason is the weather. More people _____ (retire) and they _____ (choose) warm sunny climates near the coast. Finally, many new immigrants _____ (decide) to live in the South and the West. Many new immigrants already have family and friends in these areas and it is easier to find a job.

B Dictation   Listen and write the sentences you hear.

CD 1; Track 22

1. _____

2. _____

3. _____

4. _____

5. _____

6. _____

C Tense Contrast   Circle the verb in the correct tense: simple present or present continuous.

1. Every ten years, the United States (takes/is taking) a census of the population.

2. When people move, they usually (stay/are staying) in the same state.

3. Family life (changes/is changing).

4. Almost 25% of Americans (live/is living) alone.

5. New York (grows/is growing) slowly.

PRONUNCIATION

CD 1; Track 23

Pronunciation Note: Years and numbers

It takes practice to understand and say years and large numbers.

Years

1950	nineteen fifty
1980	nineteen eighty
2000	two thousand
2004	two thousand four
2010	twenty ten

Numbers

400,000	four hundred thousand
20,400,000	twenty million, four hundred thousand
120,400,000	one hundred twenty million, four hundred thousand

CD 1; Track 23

Ⓐ Listen and Complete   The chart shows the population of the United States from 1900 to 2006. Listen and complete the information. You will hear each sentence twice.

Year	Population	Year	Population
1900	76,100,000	1960	
1910	92,400,000	1970	
1920		1980	
1930		1990	
1940		2000	
1950		2006	

Ⓑ Partner Practice   Sit with a partner. Practice asking and answering questions about the population chart.

Example: A: What was the population in <u>1970?</u>

B: It was <u>two hundred and five million, one hundred thousand.</u>

LISTENING 3: HOW DO YOU LIKE IT HERE?

CD 1; Track 24

Ⓐ Listen and Decide   Listen to the conversations about how people feel about the area they are living in. Decide if the speaker is going to stay in the same area or to move. Check *Stay* or *Move*.

Conversation	Stay	Move
1	_____	_____
2	_____	_____
3	_____	_____
4	_____	_____
5	_____	_____
6	_____	_____

CD 1; Track 24

Ⓑ Note-Taking   Listen to the conversations again. Write the city or state where each person is living now. In one or two words, write the reason this person wants to stay or move.

Conversation	Place	Reason
1	_____	_____
2	_____	_____
3	_____	_____
4	_____	_____
5	_____	_____
6	_____	_____

SPEAKING

Ⓐ Interview   Interview a classmate about living in this state. Write a few notes in the chart.

1. Do you like (<u>city, state</u>)?	
2. Why? (Why not?)	
3. Is your family here?	
4. How long have you lived in this state?	
5. Do you ever think about moving?	
6. Where would you move? Why?	

B **Population Map** Work with a partner. The map below shows several major cities in the United States.

STUDENT A: Ask Student B about the population of these cities. Write the population on the line under each city. Then change roles. Student B will ask questions about the population of the cities on the map.

STUDENT B: Turn to page 152 for the population of each city in 2007.

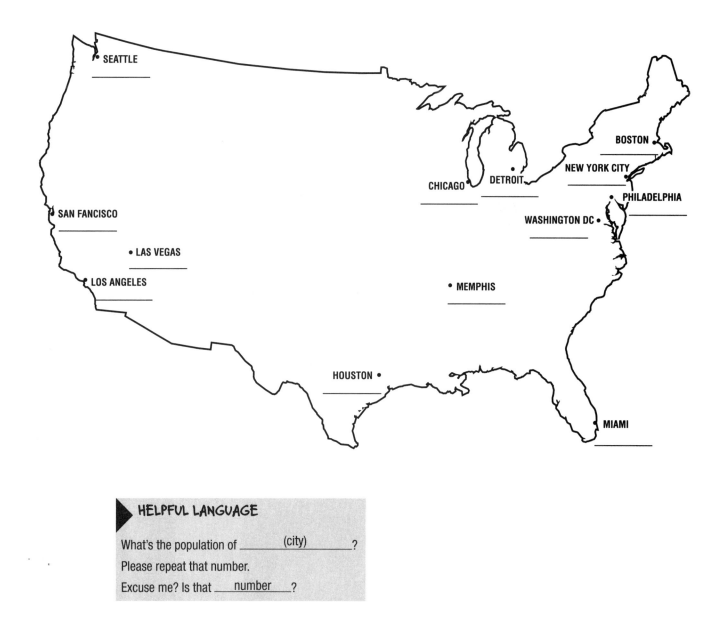

> **HELPFUL LANGUAGE**
>
> What's the population of _____(city)_____ ?
> Please repeat that number.
> Excuse me? Is that _____number_____ ?

C Write Each year, over one million people move to the United States. It is sometimes difficult for them to choose which town or city to live in. A family from your country is going to emigrate to the United States. Should they consider the area you live in? Write three things you like about your area. Write three things you don't like. Sit in a small group and share your ideas.

I like . . .

_____

_____

_____

I don't like . . .

_____

_____

_____

INTERNET ACTIVITY

A Searching for Information Look at the current census information at www.census.gov. Complete the following information.

1. The current population of the United States is _____.

2. The state with the highest population is _____. The population is _____.

3. Choose one state. What is the current population?

   State: _____

   Population: _____

STARTING YOUR OWN BUSINESS

BEFORE YOU LISTEN

A **Discuss and Check** The man in the picture is planning to start his own business as a handyman. These are some of the characteristics of a successful small business owner. Why is each of these characteristics important for him? Which of these characteristics do you think is important when owning your own business? Check all that apply.

A successful small business owner:

1. has a specific skill or ability.   _____

2. is organized and plans carefully.   _____

3. is hardworking.   _____

4. likes to be the boss.   _____

5. is a good decision maker.   _____

6. has a lot of energy.   _____

7. is confident.   _____

8. is dependable.   _____

9. can get along with people.   _____

LISTENING 1: THREE SMALL BUSINESS OWNERS

CD 2; Track 1

Ⓐ Listen and Identify Each person is a successful small business owner. Listen as each speaker describes his/her job. What is each person's job? Write two or three characteristics that make this person successful with their business.

1.

Job: _____

Characteristics:

_____

_____

_____

2.

Job: _____

Characteristics:

_____

_____

_____

3.

Job: _____

Characteristics:

_____

_____

_____

VOCABULARY

A Key Words   Discuss the new vocabulary. Then, complete the sentences.

handyman	a person who knows how to fix many things in a house
permit	an official document or license
sign	a poster or notice that gives information
supplies	materials and equipment needed to do a job
hardware	tools and small building supplies
advertisement	a sign or information to sell a product or service
to handle	to take care of

1. There is a _____ in the store window that says "Help Wanted."

2. I buy all my office _____ on the Internet.

3. There are many _____ for local businesses in the newspaper.

4. We're going to call a _____ to put a new cabinet in the bathroom.

5. All businesses need a _____ to have a store or company in this town.

6. My company is so busy that we can't _____ all the new orders.

7. You can buy everything you need to renovate your kitchen at the _____ store.

B Apply the Vocabulary   Complete the sentences.

1. Name two kinds of permits:

   _____   _____

2. Name two things you can buy at a hardware store:

   _____   _____

3. Name two supplies you need to install a window:

   _____   _____

4. Write the words from one sign in your school:

   _____

LISTENING 2: Mr. FIX-IT

> ### Listening Note: Looking at charts and checklists
>
> Speakers sometimes use charts and checklists to help their listeners follow the main ideas. As they talk, they will point to the words or ideas so that you can listen and read the chart at the same time.

A Using a Checklist   Listen as Jake describes the handyman business he is planning to start. Read the *Checklist for Starting a New Business*. Check each item as Jake speaks about it to help you follow the main ideas.

Checklist for Starting a New Business:

☐ Think about your skills and interests

☐ Decide on a starting date

☐ Decide on a business location

☐ Talk to a lawyer

☐ Apply for a business identification number

☐ Obtain a business license or permit

☐ Apply for insurance

☐ Start a business checking account

☐ Order business forms and cards

☐ Advertise the new business

B Listen and Check   Listen to Jake speak again about his business plans. Place a check in the correct column: *He did it.* or *He is going to do it.*

	He did it.	He's going to do it.
1. Speak with his boss		
2. Quit his job		
3. Buy a truck		
4. See a lawyer		
5. Get a business permit		
6. Get accident insurance		
7. Start a bank account		
8. Order business cards		
9. Advertise his new business		

Listening Note: Listening for details

After a speaker gives a main idea, he usually follows it with examples, details, or more specific information.

CD 2; Track 2

❻ Listening for Details   Listen again as Jake describes his business plans. Write one detail about each of his plans. Then, sit with a partner and share your information.

Think about your skills and experience: **He can fix anything.**

Decide on a business location: _____

Decide on a starting date: _____

Talk to a lawyer: _____

Apply for insurance: _____

Start a business checking account: _____

Order business forms: _____

Get business cards: _____

Advertise the new business: _____

❼ Discuss   Sit in a small group and talk about the questions.

1. How much experience does Jake have in the construction business?

2. Why does he feel confident that his business is going be successful?

3. Why did he need to see a lawyer?

4. Does Jake need a business permit?

5. How many days a week do you think he is going to work?

6. About how much money do you think he will need to start his business?

7. Do you think he's going to need to advertise more?

8. Look back at page 45. What characteristics of a successful small business owner do you think Jake has?

STRUCTURE

A **Future Tense**   Complete the sentences. Use the future tense with *be going to*. Some verbs may be used twice.

say	paint	order	do	send
give	work	start	begin	

1. I __**am going to work**__ at my present job for four more weeks.

2. I _____ a small business.

3. I _____ seven days a week.

4. The shop _____ a sign on my truck.

5. The sign _____ *Mr. Fix-It*.

6. The insurance _____ next month.

7. The bank _____ me checks.

8. I _____ estimates on Saturdays.

9. I _____ business forms and business cards.

10. I _____ business cards to all my friends.

B **Complete**   What will Jake say to each homeowner? Use *will* and one of the verbs from the box. Some verbs can be used more than once. Replace the underlined word(s) in each sentence with *it* or *them*.

paint	install	fix	tile	build	repair

1. The <u>garage door</u> is broken. _____**I will fix it.**_____

2. We would like <u>a new deck</u>. _____

3. We have some <u>new cabinets</u> for the kitchen.

   _____

4. I bought some new tile for the <u>bathroom floor</u>.

   _____

5. <u>The windows</u> are broken. _____

6. The paint <u>in the bedroom</u> is very old. _____

7. We have <u>a small hole in the roof</u>. _____

8. I would like <u>some shelves</u> in our garage. _____

PRONUNCIATION

CD 2; Track 3

> ## Pronunciation Note: *going to - gonna*
>
> In spoken English, *going* to sounds like *gonna*.
>
> He's *going to* order business cards.
> He's *gonna* order business cards.
>
> I'm *going to* start my own business.
> I'm *gonna* start my own business.
>
> When writing, always write *going to*; do not write *gonna*.

CD 2; Track 3

A **Listen and Repeat**   Listen and repeat the sentences.

1. Jake is going to start his own business.

2. He's going to begin next month.

3. He's going to work very hard.

4. I'm going to call Jake.

5. He's going to give me an estimate for a new kitchen window.

CD 2; Track 4

B **Dictation**   Listen and write the sentences you hear.

1. _____

2. _____

3. _____

4. _____

5. _____

6. _____

C **Partner Practice**   Sit with a partner and practice saying the sentences from Exercise B. Then, ask and answer the questions below. Try to use *gonna*.

1. What are you going to do after school?

2. What time is this class going to finish?

3. When are you going to do your homework?

4. What are you going to do tonight?

5. What time are you going to go to sleep?

6. What are you going to do this weekend?

7. When are you going to take a vacation?

LISTENING 3: THE CUSTOMERS

A Listen for Information   Listen to each conversation between Jake and a customer. Which job does the customer need Jake to do? Listen again and write the starting date on the first line under the picture. Write the price estimate on the second line.

_____   _____   _____

_____   _____   _____

SPEAKING

A Label and Discuss   Sit in a group and label each worker. Talk about the kinds of jobs that each worker does.

locksmith	exterminator	electrician
landscaper	plumber	handyman

_____   _____   _____

_____   _____   _____

B Complete the Chart Sit in a group and discuss home repairs that you needed in the past year or two. Complete the chart with information about your group members.

What kind of worker did you call?

What job did the person do?

How long did it take the person to complete this job?

How much did the job cost?

Worker	Job	Time	Cost

C Discuss Talk about these questions in a small group.

1. What skills, abilities, and experience do you have? What are your interests?

2. What kind of business would you like to start?

3. Would you prefer to work for a company or start your own business?

4. How much does it cost to start a business?

5. What are some problems that a small business might have?

6. What are some advantages of having your own business?

⏵ Complete the Information   Sit in a group of three or four students. You are partners and you are going to start a small business. Complete the information.

Type of business: _____

Name of business: _____

Location: _____

Competitors: _____

We will need $_____ to start the business.

We will need the following equipment and supplies:

_____

_____

_____

Types of advertising: _____

_____

Employees needed: _____

JOBS FOR
THE FUTURE

BEFORE YOU LISTEN

Ⓐ Discuss Discuss the occupations in the photos. Use the information below to discuss the kind of job training or education you think each person needs.

Job Training or Education

1. On-the-job-training – a person can learn the work on the job
2. High school diploma
3. Vocational or technical school or special training
4. Associate degree from a two-year college
5. Bachelor's degree from a four-year college
6. Advanced degree

B Job Outlook   Answer questions 1 to 5 about your job or the job of someone you know. Several students should report their answers to the class. Then, write two jobs in each box below. If a job has a good outlook, the number of workers and the number of jobs will be about the same. If a job has a poor outlook, there will be more workers than jobs. It will be difficult to find a job.

1. Where do you work? _____

2. What do you do? _____

3. How is business? _____ slow _____ regular _____ busy

4. Is your company hiring new workers? _____

5. Is your company laying off people? _____

Jobs with a Good Outlook	*Jobs with a Poor Outlook*
_____	_____
_____	_____

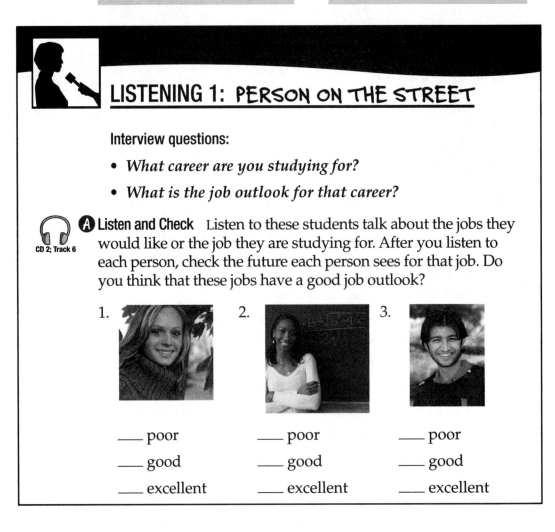

LISTENING 1: PERSON ON THE STREET

Interview questions:

- *What career are you studying for?*
- *What is the job outlook for that career?*

A Listen and Check   Listen to these students talk about the jobs they would like or the job they are studying for. After you listen to each person, check the future each person sees for that job. Do you think that these jobs have a good job outlook?

CD 2; Track 6

1.

_____ poor
_____ good
_____ excellent

2.

_____ poor
_____ good
_____ excellent

3.

_____ poor
_____ good
_____ excellent

VOCABULARY

A Key Words   Discuss the new vocabulary. Then, complete the sentences.

above average	more than usual
below average	less or fewer than usual
to be in demand	to have a need for
to increase	to become larger, to go up in number, to grow
industry	a business that makes and sells products
opening	new position or job in a company
on the other hand	in contrast, opposite
to retire	to stop working, usually when a person is 65

1. Airports, businesses, and schools are concerned about security, so the job outlook for security guards is _____.

2. My father is 64. He is going to _____ next year.

3. In the United States, many workers in the automobile _____ are losing their jobs.

4. As the population gets older, nurses will be _____.

5. Our company has an _____ for a computer programmer.

6. Each year the population _____ by more than a million people.

7. Because of technology and automatic voice recognition, the job outlook for telephone operators is _____.

8. It's difficult to find a job as a history teacher. _____, it's easy to find a job as a math teacher.

B Job Outlook Vocabulary   Put these words into two groups.

good job outlook	above average outlook	increase in jobs
few job openings	poor job outlook	number of jobs is falling
decrease in jobs	below average outlook	many job openings
	number of jobs is growing	

There will be more jobs:	There will be fewer jobs:
good job outlook	poor job outlook

LISTENING 2: JOBS FOR THE FUTURE

Listening Note: Listening for the Main Idea
Some talks are well organized. At the beginning of the talk, the speaker will tell you what the talk is about and how the talk will be organized.

A **Listen for the Main Idea**   Listen to the beginning of the talk. Complete the information.

CD 2; Track 7

1. The speaker will talk about _____ for _____ jobs.

2. It will also explain the _____.

3. The speaker got the information from the *Occupational _____ Handbook*.

B **Listen and Check**   You will hear about the job outlook for seven occupations. Listen and check the job outlook for each. After you listen, tell the class any other information you remember about each job.

CD 2; Track 8

Occupation	Poor (Below average)	Good (Average)	Excellent (Above average)
1. bank teller			
2. computer specialist			
3. mail carrier			
4. delivery worker			
5. nurse			
6. travel agent			
7. teacher			

Listening Note: Listening for Details
After you understand how the talk is organized and you know the main ideas, you can listen for the details.

C Note-Taking   Listen to the information again. Write the reason that there will be fewer or more jobs for each occupation. Write the reason in three or four words.

Occupation	Reason
1. bank teller	_____
2. computer specialists	_____
3. mail carrier	_____
4. delivery worker	_____
5. nurse	_____
6. travel agent	_____
7. teacher	_____

D Comprehension Questions   Circle the correct answer.

1. What does the *Occupational Outlook Handbook* describe?
   a. the companies that are looking for workers
   b. the duties, salary, and outlook for many jobs
   c. only jobs that require a college education

2. Why will there be fewer job openings for bank tellers?
   a. People need to cash their paychecks.
   b. More and more people will do their banking online.
   c. There will be fewer banks.

3. The job outlook for mail carriers is poor. What does that mean?
   a. A person will easily find a job as a mail carrier.
   b. A person will probably find a job as a mail carrier.
   c. A person probably won't find a job as a mail carrier.

4. Who will travel more in the future?
   a. people who are retiring
   b. teachers
   c. workers in health care

5. Many people are using the Internet to make travel plans, so
   a. the job outlook for travel agents is below average.
   b. the job outlook for travel agents is above average.
   c. there will be a need for more travel agents to help them.

6. In what subject area will a teacher have a better opportunity to find a job?
   a. in English
   b. in math
   c. in history

Listening Note: Introducing a New Idea

In a talk, the speaker can introduce each new idea, fact, or part of the talk in several ways:

1. with words such as *first, next, finally*
2. with an introductory statement
3. with a question

E Introducing a New Idea   Listen to the talk again and complete the sentences. Each sentence introduces the next part of the talk.

CD 2; Track 8

1. **Let's begin with** _____ bank tellers.

2. _____, computer workers.

3. _____ the men and women who deliver our mail?

4. _____, _____ for delivery workers is above average.

5. _____ is health care workers.

6. _____ for travel agents?

7. _____, _____ for teachers is good.

STRUCTURE

A Dictation   Listen and write the sentences you hear.

CD 2; Track 9

1. _____

2. _____

3. _____

4. _____

5. _____

6. _____

B Tense Contrast   Complete the sentences with the correct form of the verb. Use the future tense or the present continuous tense.

1. Many teachers _____ in the next ten years. (retire)

2. In the future, many people _____ their banking online. (do)

3. People _____ now _____ more items on the Internet. (buy)

4. Many people are studying nursing because there _____ many jobs in the health area. (be)

5. Because the population is growing, the number of students _____. (increase)

6. People _____ longer. (live)

7. People _____ now _____ more because the cost of an airline ticket is down. (travel)

8. My grandparents _____ a trip to Alaska next summer. (take)

9. In the future, there _____ many jobs for nurses in big city hospitals. (be)

10. My brother is studying computer technology. He _____ (find) a good job after he graduates.

PRONUNCIATION

CD 2; Track 10

Pronunciation Note: Salaries

It will take time and practice to be able to say salaries in English.

$28,000	twenty eight thousand a year
$450/week	four hundred fifty dollars a week
$20/hour	twenty dollars an hour
$9.50/hour	nine-fifty an hour

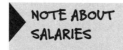

NOTE ABOUT SALARIES

All employers must pay their employees minimum wage. What is the minimum wage in your state?

A **Listen for Numbers**   This is a list of the average salary for eight jobs. Listen and complete the information. You will hear each sentence twice.

Job	Salary
1. bank teller	$18,000-$24,000
2. computer support specialist	_____
3. mail carrier	_____
4. delivery worker	_____
5. licensed practical nurse	_____
6. registered nurse	_____
7. travel agent	_____
8. teacher	_____

B **Salaries**   Look at the following information about salaries. Sit with a partner and form sentences about each job. Help each other say the numbers correctly.

Examples:

The average salary for a plumber is about $20.00 an hour.

A plumber makes about $20 an hour.

A plumber earns about $20 an hour.

The average salary for an accountant is between $40,000 and $67,000.

Job	Salary
Plumber	$20 an hour
Accountant	$40,000 - $67,000
X-ray technician	$43,000
Police officer	$45,000
Hair stylist	$20,000
Dental hygienist	$28.00 an hour
Real estate agent	$24,000 - $58,000
Truck driver	$18.00 an hour

LISTENING 3: HOW'S BUSINESS?

A Listen and Check   Listen to each speaker talk about his or her job. Check if the speaker is *working* or *not working*.

Conversation	Working	Not Working
1	_____	_____
2	_____	_____
3	_____	_____
4	_____	_____
5	_____	_____
6	_____	_____

B Match   Match each sentence from the conversations with the correct meaning.

_____ 1. I hope I'm not the next.

_____ 2. I'm on unemployment.

_____ 3. How come?

_____ 4. No one is hiring.

_____ 5. Everybody got laid off.

_____ 6. I'll look into it.

_____ 7. We have a good reputation.

a. Why?

b. We all lost our jobs.

c. Companies do not need new workers.

d. I'm worried about my job.

e. People know we do a good job.

f. I'm receiving money from the government.

g. I'll get more information.

C Listen and Choose   Listen to the conversations again. Some of the speakers are worried about their jobs. Circle the conversations in which the speakers are worried about their jobs.

Conversation 1   Conversation 4

Conversation 2   Conversation 5

Conversation 3   Conversation 6

SPEAKING

A Interview   Interview a classmate who works. Take notes in the chart below.

1. Where do you work? (Name of company)
2. What do you do?
3. How long have you worked there?
4. Do you like your job?
5. Do you work part time or full time?
6. Is your company large or small?
7. About how many people work there?
8. Is your company busy?
9. Are they hiring any new workers?
10. What is the outlook for your job?

Notes

1.	
2.	
3.	
4.	
5.	
6.	
7.	
8.	
9.	
10.	

B Job Outlook Sit in a small group and discuss the outlook for these four jobs. As a group, decide on the outlook and give your reasons.

Job: _____

Outlook: _____

Reasons: _____

_____

_____

Job: _____

Outlook: _____

Reasons: _____

_____

_____

Job: _____

Outlook: _____

Reasons: _____

_____

_____

Job: _____

Outlook: _____

Reasons: _____

_____

_____

INTERNET ACTIVITIES

Ⓐ *Occupational Outlook Handbook*   Search for the *Occupational Outlook Handbook* on the Internet. Look up a job you are interested in. Complete the following information and tell your classmates about the job.

Job: _____

Job duties: _____

_____

_____

Education: _____

Salary (Earnings): _____

Job outlook: _____

Ⓑ **Search for Salaries**   Every year, salaries change. Use the *Occupational Outlook Handbook* or another online resource and check on the salaries of several of the jobs in this unit. What is the current salary? Discuss your findings with the class.

A PROFESSIONAL

BEFORE YOU LISTEN

A **Identify the Pictures** These pictures show six types of crime. Write the name of the crime and the criminal under each picture.

mugger	vandal	car theft	robber
shoplifter	thief	robbery	vandalism
car thief	shoplifting	mugging	theft

1. __shoplifting__
   __shoplifter__

2. _____
   _____

3. _____
   _____

4. _____
   _____

5. _____
   _____

6. _____
   _____

B **Discuss** Robbery is the most common crime. What are eight common items a thief or robber will steal from a house?

LISTENING 1: PERSON ON THE STREET

Interview question:

- *Were you ever robbed?*

A Listen for Details Listen to each person describe a robbery. Where was each person when the robbery happened? On the line below each speaker, write two things that the robber took.

CD 2; Track 13

1.
2.
3.

_____ _____ _____

_____ _____ _____

B Identify the Speaker Read each statement. Then, listen to each speaker again. Write the number of the correct speaker next to each statement.

CD 2; Track 13

_____ a. The robber was in a car.

_____ b. The robber got into the house through the side door.

_____ c. This person was home when a robber got into the house.

_____ d. The robber took a leather jacket.

_____ e. The robber didn't have time to take anything.

_____ f. The robber ate some cookies that were in the house!

_____ g. The robber made a terrible mess in this house.

_____ h. This person called the police.

_____ i. The robber took jewelry and money.

_____ j. The robber broke into more than one home.

68   **Now Hear This!**

VOCABULARY

A **Key Words** Discuss the new vocabulary. Then, complete the sentences below.

typical	regular; the same as usual
briefcase	a bag for carrying business papers
screwdriver	a tool to put screws in and take them out
to climb	to go up or down, often using the hands and feet
silverware	silver spoons, knives, and forks
necklace	a piece of jewelry that is worn around the neck

1. She wore a beautiful gold _____ with her dress.

2. Please put the plates and the _____ on the table.

3. A business man or woman carries a _____ to work.

4. The thief _____ in the window.

5. The thief used a _____ to open the window.

6. On a _____ day, he leaves his house at 8:00.

B **Apply the Vocabulary** Circle the correct word.

1. Many clothing stores use security cameras to stop (shoplifter/shoplifting).

2. This building is very safe. We have never had a (rob/robbery) here.

3. The (vandalism/vandals) broke all the windows in the new house.

4. The (mugging/mugger) pushed me down and took my laptop.

5. A (thief/theft) stole my purse from my office. I reported the (thief/theft) to the security guards.

6. The (shoplifter/shoplifting) stole a watch from the store.

7. Most (robbers/robberies) prefer to work at night when people are out.

8. There were fifty (muggers/muggings) in this city last month.

LISTENING 2: A PROFESSIONAL

CD 2; Track 14

A Order the Pictures   Look at the pictures below and listen to the story about a professional thief. As you listen, number the pictures in the correct order from 1 to 6. After you listen, retell the information you remember about each picture.

☐   ☐

☐   ☐

☐   ☐

CD 2; Track 14

B Listen for Details   Listen to the story again. Write the names of the five items Richard stole from this house.

1. _____   4. _____

2. _____   5. _____

3. _____

> **Listening Note: Following a news story**
> When you hear about an event in the news, ask yourself the *Wh* questions: *What happened, Who, Where, When, Why,* and *How.* This will help you learn about the key details of a news story.

C Wh- questions   Listen to the story again and answer the *Wh-* questions.

1. What happened?

2. Who did it?

3. Where did this happen?

4. When did it happen?

5. Why did he choose this house?

6. How did the thief get into the house?

D Comprehension Questions   Circle the letter of the correct answer.

1. Why did Richard wear a business suit?
   a. because he's a professional
   b. because he didn't want anyone to look at him
   c. because he works hard

2. What did Richard do after the man left the house?
   a. He entered the house.
   b. He stood behind a tree.
   c. He walked around the block again.

3. Why did Richard choose this house?
   a. because he saw both the man and the woman leave the house
   b. because the house is in an expensive area
   c. because the man was wearing a business suit

4. How did Richard get into the house?
   a. He broke a window.
   b. He climbed in a window.
   c. He walked in the front door.

5. Why didn't Richard take the television set?
   a. It was too big.
   b. It was too old.
   c. He didn't need a TV.

6. How long did Richard stay in the house?
   a. five minutes
   b. fifteen minutes
   c. one hour

7. How often does Richard rob a house?
   a. every day
   b. once a month
   c. This was the first time he robbed a house.

STRUCTURE

A Dictation   Listen and write the sentences you hear.

CD 2; Track 15

1. _____

2. _____

3. _____

4. _____

5. _____

6. _____

B Past Tense   Complete these sentences from the story. Use the past tense of the verbs below.

| pass | dress | park | climb | walk | carry |
| look | open | watch | want | work | |

1. Richard ____**dressed**____ in a business suit.

2. He _____ his car in a busy area.

3. Richard _____ a briefcase.

4. He saw what he _____.

5. He _____ a woman leave the same house.

6. Richard _____ the window and _____ in.

7. Richard _____ quickly.

8. Richard _____ a TV and a computer.

9. He _____ back to his car with his briefcase.

10. No one _____ at him.

PRONUNCIATION

A *-ed* **Endings**   Say each of these past tense verbs to yourself. Before you listen, decide if the verb has one or two syllables. Write the number of syllables in the *Before* column. Then, listen to the pronunciation of each verb. Write the number of syllables you hear in the *After* column.

	Before	After			Before	After
1. parked	___	___		7. climbed	___	___
2. wanted	___	___		8. waited	___	___
3. dressed	___	___		9. walked	___	___
4. worked	___	___		10. started	___	___
5. needed	___	___		11. robbed	___	___
6. passed	___	___		12. carried	___	___

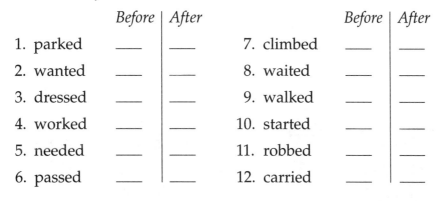

Pronunciation Note: Linking with ed

When a final *-ed* is followed by a word that begins with a vowel, the sounds are linked. The *d* sounds like part of the next word.

He watche**d a** woman leave the house.

B Linking with -ed   Listen carefully and complete these sentences with the missing words. Mark the linking sounds.

1. He ____**parked**____ __**on**__ Main Street.

2. He _____ _____ a business suit.

3. He _____ _____ the block.

4. He _____ _____ color TV.

5. He _____ _____ the morning.

6. He _____ _____ briefcase.

7. He _____ _____ window.

8. He _____ _____.

9. He _____ _____ house every day.

C Partner Practice   Sit with a partner and practice saying each sentence in Exercise B. Try to link the final sound of each verb with the following vowel.

LISTENING 3: THE END OF RICHARD'S CAREER

CD 2; Track 18

A Listen for Key Words Richard robbed homes on Monday, Tuesday, and Wednesday. Listen to the four homeowners speak to the police officer. As you listen, write three or four words under each picture to help you remember each conversation. After you listen, sit with a partner. What do you remember about each conversation? Use the words you wrote to help you remember the information.

| CONVERSATION 1 | CONVERSATION 2 | CONVERSATION 3 |
| Monday | Tuesday | Wednesday |

_____   _____   _____

_____   _____   _____

_____   _____   _____

_____   _____   _____

CD 2; Track 18

B Listen and Answer During each conversation, the police officer and the homeowners asked many questions. Listen to the conversations again. Use your notes to answer the questions.

CONVERSATION 1:

1. How did the thief get into the house?

2. What did he take?

3. Why didn't he take the computer or the television set?

CONVERSATION 2:

1. What time did you leave your home?

2. Which way did he go?

3. Did you get the license plate number?

4. Did you get a good look at him?

5. Did he take anything?

CONVERSATION 3:

1. Do you live here?

2. Where were you?

3. Did you catch him?

Listening Note: Putting Events in Order

Putting important events in order will help you follow a story from beginning to end.

C Order the Events Read these sentences about the three robberies. Listen to the conversations again. Then, put the sentences in order from 1 to 8.

_____ a. A man came into the living room and surprised him.

_____ b. The couple wasn't home, so Richard had time to take several items.

_____ c. Richard ran out the door, got into his car, and drove away.

_____ d. The owner had to return home a few minutes later.

__1__ e. On Monday, Richard broke into a house.

_____ f. The next day, he broke into another house.

_____ g. Richard broke into a third house.

_____ h. Richard ran out the door and he fell down the front steps.

SPEAKING

A Interview Sit in a small group. Interview a student who was robbed or who knows about a robbery that was recently in the news.

1. Did anyone ever rob you (or someone you know)?	
2. Where were you living?	
3. How did the thief get in the house?	
4. What time of day was it?	
5. Was anyone home?	
6. What did the thief take?	
7. Did you see the thief?	
8. Did you call the police?	
9. Did they ever catch the thief?	

B Tell the Story Last night when Lisa was sleeping, a thief broke into her apartment. In a small group, put the pictures of this robbery in order from 1 to 6. Talk about what happened. Then, as a group, write the story of the robbery.

_____

_____

_____

_____

_____

_____

_____

_____

_____

_____

_____

_____

THE LOTTERY

BEFORE YOU LISTEN

A Discuss   Write your favorite number. _____
Explain why it is your favorite number.

B Lucky Numbers   Circle the numbers below that are lucky numbers in your country. Cross out the unlucky numbers. Explain your reasons.

1	2	3	4	5	6	7	8	9	10
11	12	13	14	15	16	17	18	19	20
21	22	23	24	25	26	27	28	29	30

C Read   Read the article about the lottery. Underline and discuss any new vocabulary words.

The Lottery

In the United States, residents of 38 states and the District of Columbia can buy lottery tickets. Lotteries are run by the state and in most states, the money that comes from the lottery helps with the state education budget. In a state lottery, a person buys a ticket with numbers. The person can choose the numbers or a lottery machine can choose the numbers automatically. If the numbers on the ticket match the winning numbers, the person wins. States offer many kinds of lottery games, such as scratch-off games and games where you can choose a set of numbers.

Tens of millions of people buy lottery tickets every day, hoping to win $50,000, $100,000, one million dollars, or more. However, when a person wins a million dollars, he doesn't receive a check for the total amount. In most states, the person receives $50,000 a year for 20 years. The federal government takes 28% of that amount for taxes. In addition, the winner also must pay income taxes on the money. After taxes, a million-dollar winner receives from $25,000 to $35,000 a year for 20 years.

LISTENING 1: PERSON ON THE STREET

Interview question:

- *What would you do if you won a million dollars?*

CD 2; Track 19   **A Listen and Name**   Listen to each person dream about winning the lottery. Name two things that each person would do or buy.

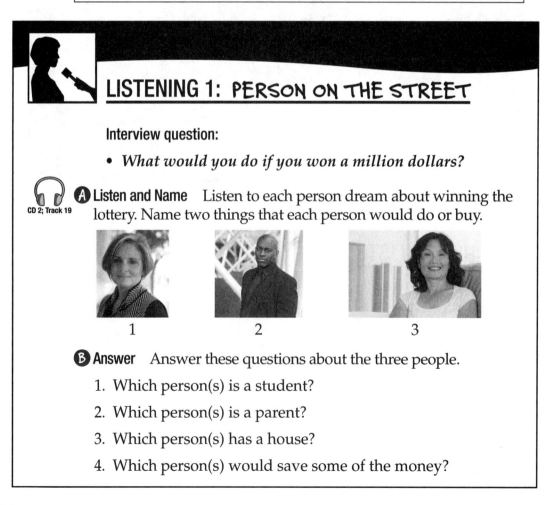

1   2   3

B Answer   Answer these questions about the three people.

1. Which person(s) is a student?

2. Which person(s) is a parent?

3. Which person(s) has a house?

4. Which person(s) would save some of the money?

VOCABULARY

Ⓐ Key Words   Discuss the new vocabulary. Then complete the sentences below.

to quit	to stop an activity, e.g. to stop working
fault	responsibility for a mistake
opportunity	chance; a good time to do or try something
bored	a feeling of not being interested
tuition	the cost of going to private school or to college
immediately	right now, without delay
security	a feeling of being safe, of not being worried

1. My father retired and he doesn't know what to do with his time. He's _____.

2. Money in the bank brings _____.
   You know that if you need it, it's there.

3. I failed the test because I didn't study for it.
   It's my _____.

4. When she saw that she had a winning lottery ticket, she
   _____ called her parents.

5. He has the _____ to travel to Japan.

6. If I won a lot of money, I would _____
   my job.

7. The _____ at that college is more than
   $20,000 year.

Ⓑ Apply the Vocabulary   Circle the correct answer.

1. You pay *tuition* to attend a _____.
   a. university   b. concert

2. If you are *bored* in class, you find it difficult
   to _____.
   a. talk with a friend   b. pay attention to the teacher

3. After two accidents, Lenny *quit* driving.
   Now, Lenny _____.
   a. takes the bus   b. drives his car

4. I never had the *opportunity* to attend college
   because _____.
   a. I had to work to   b. I wanted to study
      support my family   chemistry

5. It is Fred's *fault* that he didn't pass the math test.
   He's upset with _____.
   a. his math teacher   b. himself

LISTENING 2: LOTTERY WINNERS

Listening Note: Preparing to Listen

Before you listen, ask yourself questions about the topic. Listen for the answers. What information do you still want to know?

Ⓐ Preparing to Listen   You are going to hear about four lottery winners. What information would you like to know about each winner? Write four of your questions.

1. _____

2. _____

3. _____

4. _____

CD 2; Track 20

Ⓑ Listen for Numbers   Listen to this information about four lottery winners. As you listen, write down the number of tickets each person bought and the amount of money that each person won. After you listen, tell the class any other information you remember about the story.

	Number of tickets	Amount of money
1. Lisa K.	_____	_____
2. Mark L.	_____	_____
3. Mabel S.	_____	_____
4. Jack B.	_____	_____

CD 2; Track 20

Ⓒ Note-Taking   Listen to the story again. As you listen, take notes about what each person was doing before they won the lottery. Then, write what each person is doing now.

Name	Before	Now
1. Lisa K.		
2. Mark L.		
3. Mabel S.		
4. Jack B.		

D Answer Sit in a group and answer these questions. Use your notes to help you.

1. Who won the most money?

2. Who quit a job?

3. Which person was retired when he/she won the lottery?

4. Who didn't quit a job?

5. Who spent too much money?

6. What is Lisa studying?

7. Mark quit a job he didn't like and he has lots of money. Why isn't he happy?

8. Why is Mabel having financial problems?

9. What does Jack think about money?

E Review Your Questions Look back at your questions from Exercise A. Did the story answer all of your questions? What questions were not answered?

STRUCTURE

A Tense Contrast Complete the sentences with the simple present or past tense. All of the sentences are negative.

1. Lisa **didn't enjoy** her job. (enjoy)

2. She _____ enough money to go to school. (have)

3. She _____ at the market anymore. (work)

4. When Mark was working, he _____ time for his family. (have)

5. He _____ to sell cars again. (want)

6. Mabel _____ her money carefully. (spend)

7. She _____ enough money to pay her taxes. (have)

8. She _____ money to her grandchildren anymore. (give)

9. Jack _____ his job. (quit)

10. He _____ about sending his children to college. (worry)

B Dictation   Listen and write the sentences you hear. You will hear *doesn't* or *didn't* in each sentence.

1. _____
2. _____
3. _____
4. _____
5. _____
6. _____

PRONUNCIATION

Pronunciation Note: Linking with A/An

When a final consonant is followed by *a* or *an*, the sounds are linked. The *a* or *an* sounds like part of the word before.

He won‿a million dollars

A Linking with A/An   Complete these sentences with the missing words. Mark the linking sounds.

1. Lisa _____**was**_____ ___**a**___ cashier in a supermarket.

2. She wants to _____ _____ artist.

3. Mark _____ _____ car salesman.

4. He worked seven _____ _____ week.

5. Mabel stopped _____ _____ store.

6. She _____ _____ new car.

7. Jack _____ _____ ticket.

8. He teaches _____ _____ high school.

9. They _____ _____ new car.

10. They take their children _____ _____ interesting vacation every year.

B Partner Practice   Sit with a partner and practice repeating the sentences in Exercise A. Try to link the sounds in the words that you wrote.

Pronunciation Note: Negative contractions

When listening, we often do not hear a full *t* at the end of a negative contraction.

They don't worry about money.

She didn't pay her taxes.

C Negative Contractions   Listen and write the negative contraction you hear.

1. She _____ have enough money to go to school.

2. If I _____ become an artist, it's my own fault.

3. He _____ have time for family life.

4. He _____ want to sell cars again.

5. He _____ sure what to do.

6. She _____ have any more money.

7. He _____ quit his job.

8. They _____ worry about money.

9. Money _____ bring happiness.

D Partner Practice   Sit with a partner and practice saying the sentences in Exercise C.

E Complete and Practice   Complete the sentences with information about yourself. Say your sentences to a partner. Do not say the *t* in the negative contraction.

1. I don't have a _____.

2. I didn't get up at _____.

3. I didn't bring a _____ to school today.

4. This class doesn't meet on _____.

5. I like _____ music, but I don't like _____ music.

6. Our teacher is from _____. He/She isn't from _____.

LISTENING 3: DO YOU EVER BUY LOTTERY TICKETS?

CD 2; Track 24

Ⓐ How Many? Listen to each person talk about lottery tickets and write the number of lottery tickets each person buys each week.

Conversation	Number of Tickets
1	_____
2	_____
3	_____
4	_____
5	_____
6	_____
7	_____

CD 2; Track 24

Ⓑ Match Read the statements. Listen to each conversation again and write the number of the correct conversation.

_____ a. This person used to buy lottery tickets, but he doesn't anymore.

_____ b. This person's relative won the lottery.

_____ c. This person always plays his lucky numbers.

_____ d. This person only buys tickets when the jackpot is high.

_____ e. This person wastes five dollars a week.

_____ f. This person is sure that he's going to win the lottery.

_____ g. This person won some money.

Ⓒ Same or Different Read each pair of sentences. The first sentence is from the conversation in Exercise A. Then, read the next sentence. If the meaning is the same, circle S. If the meaning is different, circle D.

1. a. I never win a penny.   S   D
   b. I don't win any money.

2. a. I still keep buying tickets.   S   D
   b. I'm not going to buy any more tickets.

3. a. They still have to eat.   S   D
   b. They need money for other expenses.

4. a. I used to buy tickets.   S   D
   b. I still buy tickets.

5. a. I never bought another ticket.   S   D
   b. I'm going to buy another ticket.

6. a. Someday it's going to be me.   S   D
   b. I'm going to win the lottery.

7. a. I buy tickets on the way home.   S   D
   b. I stop for tickets when I'm driving home.

SPEAKING

Ⓐ Interview Interview a student in your class. Take a few notes about his or her answers. Join with another group and talk about your information.

1. Are you a lucky person?	
2. Why or why not?	
3. What's your lucky number?	
4. Does this state have a state lottery?	
5. Do you ever buy lottery tickets?	
6. How many a week?	
7. Did you ever win any money?	
8. Did you ever lose any money?	
9. What would you do if you won the lottery?	

Ⓑ Choose and Explain Sit with a partner and look at the lottery form. If a person picks the correct six numbers between 1 and 49, the prize is one million dollars. Talk together and pick six numbers between 1 and 49. Circle them on the form. Tell another group your numbers. Explain how you chose your numbers.

> **HELPFUL LANGUAGE**
>
> I like that number, too.
>
> What do you think?
>
> How about number ___?
>
> I don't like that number.
>
> No, that's an unlucky number.

C Discuss   Look at this chart about the odds in life. Which odds surprise you? Discuss your opinions with the class.

1.	The odds of developing cancer	1 in 3
2.	The odds of dying from cancer	1 in 7
3.	The odds of being the victim of a serious crime	1 in 20
4.	The odds of living to be 100	1 in 50
5.	The odds of having twins	1 in 67
6.	The odds of dying in a car accident	1 in 81
7.	The odds of someone stealing your car	1 in 194
8.	The odds of becoming a professional athlete	1 in 22,000
9.	The odds of a dog biting you	1 in 132,000
10.	The odds of winning the lottery	1 in 14,000,000

D Share Your Opinion   Read the opinions of each person below. Check if you agree or disagree with each statement. Then, sit with a small group of students and discuss your opinions about each statement.

When you buy a lottery ticket, you are just throwing your money away.

☐ I agree.   ☐ I disagree.

The more you play, the more you lose. You are smarter to put your money in the bank.

☐ I agree.   ☐ I disagree.

If you are against the lottery, don't play. But, if I want to play the lottery, it's my right.

☐ I agree.   ☐ I disagree.

The lottery is a form of gambling. The government should not sponsor this kind of activity.

☐ I agree.   ☐ I disagree.

CELL PHONES

BEFORE YOU LISTEN

A Discuss Talk about the questions.

1. Do you have a cell phone?

2. Who do you talk to most often?

3. How long do you talk on your cell phone every day?

4. What is the cell phone policy in your class? in your school?

B Read and Discuss Read this article about a possible ban on cell phones when crossing the street. Then, discuss the questions below.

> **ban** – to prohibit; to forbid; to say that you cannot do something
>
> **propose** – to recommend; to advise; to suggest

Ban Proposed on Cell Phones and MP3 Players

We see it every day, people talking on their cell phones or listening to their MP3 players as they cross the street. A state senator from New York says that this is a dangerous activity. Carl Kruger, a state senator from Brooklyn, New York, introduced a bill (law) that would ban the use of cell phones and MP3 players when people are crossing the street. In his city, three people were killed when they stepped in front of cars or busses. In one case, people were screaming at a young man to watch out, but he couldn't hear them because he was wearing headphones. Mr. Kruger says that people are "tuned in" to their electronic devices and are "tuned out" to what is happening around them. If his bill becomes a law, people will receive a $100 fine if they cross the street while using an electronic device. New York was the first city to ban handheld phones by drivers. Will they be the first to ban the use of these devices when crossing the street?

Discussion Questions:

1. What do you think about this proposed law?

2. Do you use a cell phone or MP3 player when you walk along the street?

3. Do you think that people are paying attention to traffic when they are using one of these electronic devices?

LISTENING 1: PERSON ON THE STREET

Interview questions:

- *How long do you talk on your cell phone every day?*
- *Who do you talk to?*

CD 3; Track 1

A Listen for Information   Listen to each person answer the interview questions. Complete the sentences with the information you hear. After you listen to each speaker, tell the class any information you remember about the answers.

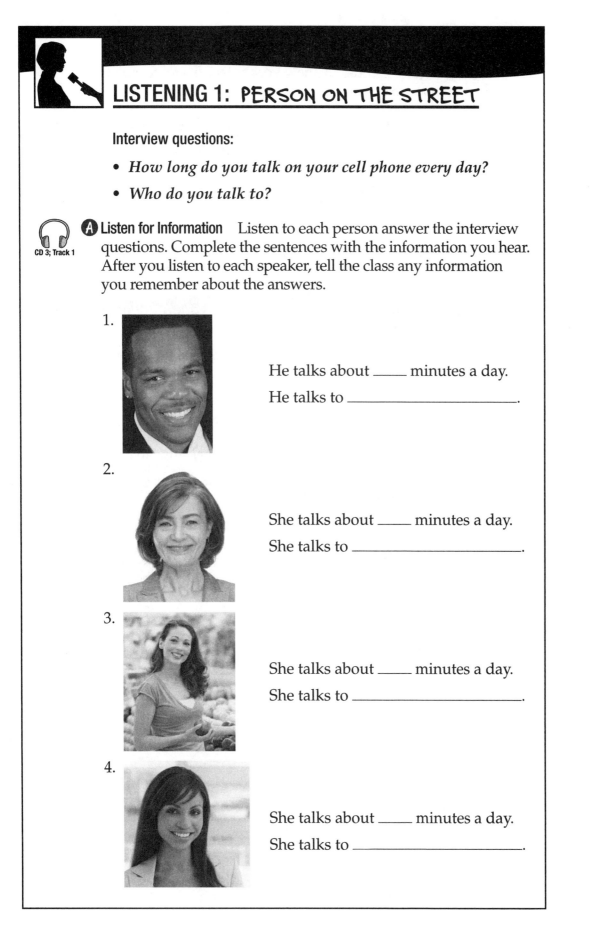

1.

He talks about _____ minutes a day.

He talks to _____.

2.

She talks about _____ minutes a day.

She talks to _____.

3.

She talks about _____ minutes a day.

She talks to _____.

4.

She talks about _____ minutes a day.

She talks to _____.

VOCABULARY

Ⓐ Key Words   Discuss the new vocabulary. Then, complete the sentences below.

a pain (in the neck)	something that annoys or bothers a person
annoyed	angry; mad; upset
to get off (the phone)	to stop talking on the phone
full	filled with people, with no empty seats or places
quietly	softly; not loud
to ban	to prohibit; to forbid
to bother	to irritate or to annoy someone

1. The teacher was _____ when one student began to talk during the test.

2. There were no tickets left for the movie. The theater was _____.

3. The baby is sleeping. Please talk _____.

4. This bus is a _____ in the neck. It never comes on time!

5. It _____ me when a cell phone rings in a restaurant.

6. The library in our town _____ the use of cell phones in the building.

7. Steve, _____ the phone now. It's time for dinner.

Ⓑ Word Web   Use the Word Web to practice new vocabulary words. Write four words about things that annoy or bother you.

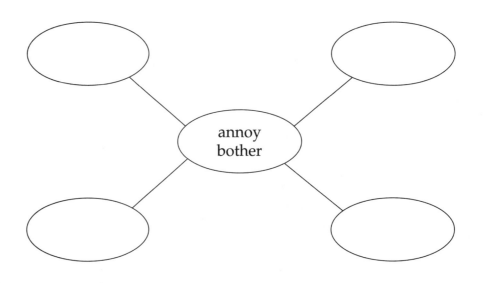

LISTENING 2: CELL PHONES, A CONVERSATION

Ⓐ Listen for Places   Some friends are talking about cell phones. As you listen, decide how many people are talking. The speakers talk about four places. As you listen, write the names of the places on the lines below. After you listen, tell the class any information you remember about the people who were talking on their cell phones.

1. _____

2. _____

3. _____

4. _____

Listening Note: Conversation Skills
When friends talk, they make comments and ask questions to show that they are listening and to be a part of the conversation.

Ⓑ Match   Read each statement (1 to 7) and the comments and expressions (a. to g.). Listen to the conversation again and write the letter of the comment or question that follows each statement.

Statements:

1. She answered her phone and started talking to a friend in the movie theater. **b**

2. And someone called out, "Get off the phone." ____

3. Pretty soon, everyone knew the color, the price . . . ____

4. All about her boyfriend. And she was talking loud. ____

5. Well, the waiter came over and asked her to talk outside. ____

6. But to sit and talk at a table in a restaurant . . . ____

7. There's now a sign in my bank: *No Cell Phones*. ____

Comments and Expressions:

a. Bravo!

b. What's wrong with people?

c. In your bank?

d. Why is it a person on a cell phone never talks quietly?

e. Some people think they can talk anywhere.

f. Some restaurants are banning cell phones.

g. Did anyone say anything?

C Continue the Conversation Write a comment or question after each statement to continue the conversation or to be a part of the conversation.

1. Our school has a cell phone policy. We have to turn off all cell phones before the class begins.
   Our school has the same policy.

2. In our town, you can't use your cell phone in the post office.

   _____

3. I was in the library . . . studying. A woman at the next table got a call and started speaking with her boyfriend. I couldn't concentrate.

   _____

4. At home, we don't have regular phone service anymore. We just use our cell phones.

   _____

5. I get great cell phone reception.

   _____

6. My cell phone is connected to the Internet. I can even get my e-mail on it.

   _____

7. In my state, it's against the law to talk on a cell phone in the car. You have to use a hands-free phone or you'll get a ticket.

   _____

8. I have 3,000 minutes on my calling plan and I sometimes go over the limit.

   _____

9. I can use my cell phone for calls in this country, but I can't make calls to my native country.

   _____

10. I had a two-year calling plan with a carrier and it's finished next month.

   _____

STRUCTURE

> ### ▶ Grammar Note: Should
> Use *should* to give advice, an opinion, or a suggestion.
> With *should,* use the simple form of the verb.
> > You should sit in the quiet car.
> >
> > A lot of places should ban cell phones.

Ⓐ Complete with Should   Complete the sentences with *should* and the correct verb.

put	ban	call	turn off
use	speak	buy	pay attention

1. You _____**should call**_____ me when you have the information.

2. People _____ softly when they use their cell phones.

3. Drivers _____ hands-free cell phones.

4. You _____ your cell phone before class.

5. The movie theater _____ all cell phone use.

6. In restaurants, movie theaters, and other public places, you _____ your cell phone on *vibrate.*

7. My parents don't have a cell phone. They _____ one in case of any emergency.

8. People _____ when they are using a cell phone when crossing the street.

Ⓑ Write   As a class, write four rules of safety or of etiquette (polite behavior) that cell phone users should follow.

1. **If you get a call at a restaurant, you should leave the table to speak.**

2. _____

3. _____

4. _____

5. _____

PRONUNCIATION

CD 3; Track 3

Pronunciation Note: Word stress

In a conversation, people stress words that are important or that give their story special emphasis. Stressed words are said longer and more loudly.

CD 3; Track 3

Ⓐ Word Stress Listen and underline the stressed word or words in each sentence. After you complete the exercise, sit with a partner. Take turns reading the sentences, giving emphasis to the underlined words.

1. She answered the phone and started talking to a friend in the movie theater.

2. What's wrong with people?

3. He called everyone he knew and told them the same story, the same information about his car.

4. Well, how about restaurants?

5. A person on a cell phone never talks quietly.

6. I know. They talk so loud.

7. Well, the waiter came over and asked her to talk outside.

8. I can understand if it's an emergency.

9. There's now a sign in my bank: *No Cell Phones.*

Ⓑ Partner Practice Stay with your partner. Read each sentence. Underline the word or words *you* would stress. Say your sentences, stressing the words you underlined.

1. My daughter is on her cell phone all day.

2. That ring tone is driving me crazy!

3. If you talk in your car, you should use a hands-free phone.

4. I only use a cell phone for emergencies.

5. My brother talks on his cell phone for over two hours a day.

6. My cell phone gets terrible reception.

7. Turn off your cell phone before class begins.

8. They now ban cell phones at my gym.

LISTENING 3: TELEPHONE CONVERSATIONS

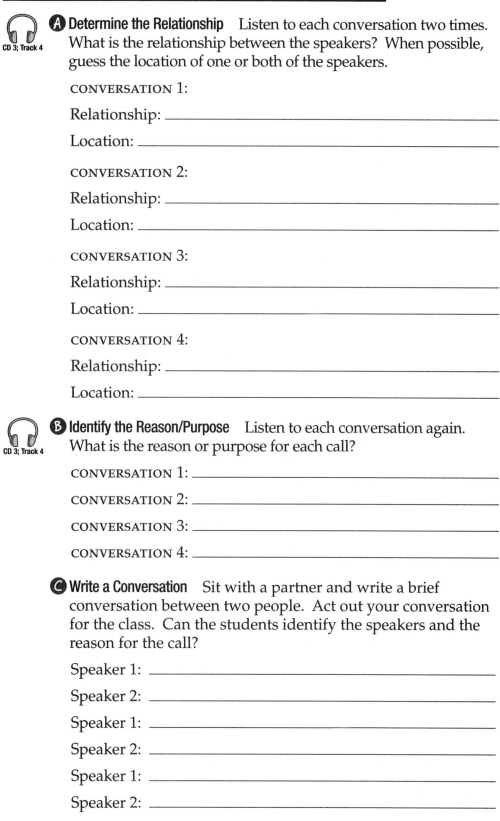

A **Determine the Relationship**   Listen to each conversation two times. What is the relationship between the speakers? When possible, guess the location of one or both of the speakers.

CONVERSATION 1:

Relationship: _____

Location: _____

CONVERSATION 2:

Relationship: _____

Location: _____

CONVERSATION 3:

Relationship: _____

Location: _____

CONVERSATION 4:

Relationship: _____

Location: _____

B **Identify the Reason/Purpose**   Listen to each conversation again. What is the reason or purpose for each call?

CONVERSATION 1: _____

CONVERSATION 2: _____

CONVERSATION 3: _____

CONVERSATION 4: _____

C **Write a Conversation**   Sit with a partner and write a brief conversation between two people. Act out your conversation for the class. Can the students identify the speakers and the reason for the call?

Speaker 1: _____

Speaker 2: _____

Speaker 1: _____

Speaker 2: _____

Speaker 1: _____

Speaker 2: _____

SPEAKING

Ⓐ Complete and Discuss Sit in a small group. Check the features you have on your cell phone. Which ones do you use? Discuss your selections with the members of your group.

_____ I can text message.   _____ I can get directions.

_____ I can talk hands-free.   _____ I can check the weather.

_____ I can get my e-mail.   _____ I can make a conference call.

_____ I can connect to   _____ I can watch video
     the Internet.   and movies.

_____ I can take photos.   _____ I can dial a number
                                             with my voice.

_____ I can listen to music.   _____ I can call anywhere in
                                             the world.

_____ I can listen to   _____ I can use my phone as
     the radio.   a credit card.

What other features does your cell phone have?

1. _____

2. _____

Ⓑ Complete the Chart Sit in a small group of three or four students. Complete the chart with the information about the phone plans of three students. Then, answer the questions on the next page.

	Student 1:	Student 2:	Student 3:
Company			
Number of phones			
Number of minutes			
Areas included			
Quality of reception			
Cost			

1. Who has the most minutes on his/her plan?

2. Who has the most phones?

3. Who can talk anywhere in the country?

4. Who gets the best reception?

5. Who pays the most for his/her plan?

6. Who pays the least for his/her plan?

7. Who is the most satisfied with his/her plan?

C Discuss and Decide   More and more places are banning cell phones. In a small group, decide if people should be able to use their cell phones in each of these locations. Give your reasons. Add two more places that you think should ban cell phone use.

1. restaurants

2. classrooms

3. museums

4. movie theaters

5. supermarkets

6. post offices

7. banks

8. movie theaters

9. busses

10. libraries

11. health clubs

12. hospitals

13. _____

14. _____

D Identify the Meaning   Many people send text messages on their phones. Follow the directions below and complete each part of the exercise .

Part 1.   Match the text message and the words.

____ 1. HAND   a. Got to go

____ 2. SRY   b. I see

____ 3. MUSM   c. Sorry

____ 4. G2G   d. You'll be sorry

____ 5. YBS   e. Miss you so much

____ 6. IC   f. All my love

____ 7. AML   g. Have a nice day

Part 2.   In a group, try to guess the meaning of this text.

1. RUOK _____

2. PLZ _____

3. OIC _____

4. THX _____

5. CUL8R _____

6. B4N _____

7. PCM _____

INTERNET ACTIVITY

A Search for Words   Use the Internet to find five more text message words or phrases and their meanings. Write the phrases and their meanings on the lines below.

_____

_____

_____

_____

_____

CARJACKINGS

BEFORE YOU LISTEN

Ⓐ Read   Read the information about carjackings. Underline and discuss new vocabulary.

Carjacking

Carjacking is a crime in which someone steals a car when a person is in it or is getting into it. Each year, there are about 35,000 carjackings in the United States. About one of every 5,000 people is the victim of a carjacking.

Carjacking is a violent crime. In 77 percent of the carjackings in the United States, the carjacker uses a weapon. Victims are injured in about 25 percent of carjackings. Some are injured by a weapon, but others are hurt when they are pushed or pulled from the car. Carjackings most often occur at night. Most carjackers are men, and in half of these crimes, two or more men work together. They often steal cars as a "business" and may receive up to $1,000 a car. The three most commonly stolen cars are Honda Accord™, Honda Civic™, and Toyota Camry™.

Police offer many tips to prevent a carjacking. Drive with your doors locked and wear a seatbelt. Park in a well-lighted area. If you see someone approaching you, move away from your car and return to a store, gas station, or other building. If a person is about to grab you, throw your keys away from you and away from the carjacker. Hopefully, the carjacker will go after your keys and you will be able to run in the other direction.

B Check   Read the sentences. Check the sentences that are true.

You are more likely to be the victim of a carjacking if you

a. park in a dark area. ____

b. lock your car doors. ____

c. drive a Honda Civic™. ____

d. often go to the store at night. ____

e. wear your seatbelt. ____

LISTENING 1: PERSON ON THE STREET

Interview Question:

- *When you get in your car, do you lock the doors right away?*

A Listen for Information   Listen to each person answer the question.

CD 3; Track 5

1

3

2

4

As you listen, complete the information below.

This person always locks the car doors.   ____   and   ____

This person sometimes locks the car doors.   ____

This person never locks the car door.   ____

VOCABULARY

A Key Words   Discuss the new vocabulary. Then, complete the sentences.

wallet	a small case where people keep money and credit cards
cashier	a person who works in a store and takes payment from customers
to lock	to secure, such as lock a door
lucky	having good luck; fortunate
grocery	a food store
reverse	a car gear a driver uses to back up the car
you're kidding	An expression of surprise; also: "You aren't serious!" "Really?"
to yell	to call out or shout very loud, often in anger or when help is needed

1. He bought some rice and milk at the _____.

2. He gave the _____ a ten dollar bill and she gave him $6.00 change.

3. He put the money in his _____.

4. Please _____ the door when you leave the house.

5. _____! They're going to get married? They just met last month!

6. She put the car in _____ and backed out of the garage.

7. She _____ for help when a man tried to take her bags.

8. My father was _____ yesterday. He found $100 on the street!

B Apply the Vocabulary   Circle two words that you can associate with each vocabulary word.

1. reverse: go backward   back up   go forward

2. yell: shout   talk softly   scream

3. grocery: food   police   supermarket

4. kidding: children   joking   teasing

5. lock: close   open   fasten

6. wallet: money   room   credit cards

LISTENING 2: TWO CARJACKINGS

 A Listen and Match   You are going to hear two stories about carjackings. Listen and decide which picture each story is describing. Then, tell the class any information you remember about the stories.

| _____ Story 1   _____ Story 2 | _____ Story 1   _____ Story 2 |

 Listening Note: Tone of Voice
Sometimes, you cannot see the speaker, but the tone of voice, vocabulary, and expressions can give you an idea of the age of the speaker and who he/she is talking to.

 B Tone of Voice   Listen to each story again. Complete the information below. Then, talk about the reasons for your guesses.

Story 1:

How old do you think the speaker is?_____

Who do you think he is talking to?   _____

Story 2:

How old do you think the speaker is?_____

Who do you think she is talking to?   _____

Listening Note: Like, you see, uh, well

In informal conversation, people often pause, repeat words, and use expressions such as *well, like, you see,* and *uh.* These extra words do not have any meaning. They are pauses and they give the speaker time to think.

CD 3; Track 7

C "Extra" Words   These sentences have several "extra" words. Listen and give the idea of each sentence. (Do not complete the sentences.)

1. Well, see, _____ like . . . uh, _____ or something.

2. And then _____ like, _____ or something _____.

3. So, _____ and _____ you know, _____.

4. And then, like, these two guys _____.

D Order the Events   These sentences describe the carjacking attempt at the gas station. Put the sentences in order from 1 to 10.

____ A man came up to her car and showed her a five-dollar bill.

_**2**_ She checked her wallet and saw that she had a ten-dollar bill.

____ Then, the man tried to get into her car.

____ She got back in her car and locked the door.

_**1**_ A woman drove into a gas station.

____ He said, "You dropped this in the store."

____ The woman drove to the police station and reported what happened.

____ She put $10 worth of gas into her car.

____ She answered, "That's not mine."

____ She went into the store and paid for the gas.

STRUCTURE

A Dictation   Listen and write the sentences you hear.

CD 3; Track 8

1. _____

2. _____

3. _____

4. _____

5. _____

6. _____

B Past Tense   First, write each verb in the box in the past tense. Then, fill in the newspaper account of the attempted car jacking.

pay	_____	return	_____	say	_____
answer	_____	try	_____	stop	_____
drive	_____	give	_____	lock	_____
get	_____	report	_____	walk	_____
drop	_____	show	_____		

On April 19th, a local woman _____ at the gas station on Park Avenue in Westin. She _____ gas, _____ for the gas inside the store, then _____ to her car. When she got into her car, she _____ the doors. A well-dressed man _____ up to her car and _____ her a five-dollar bill. He _____, "You _____ this in the store." When she _____ that it was not her money, the man _____ to get into her car. The woman immediately _____ to the police station and _____ the incident to the police. She also _____ the police a good description of the man. An artist's picture of this man is now in all area gas stations and stores. If you see this man, please call the police.

PRONUNCIATION

CD 3; Track 9

> ## Pronunciation: h in his, him, and her
> We hear the *h* in *his, him,* and *her* when it is the first word in a sentence.
> We often do not hear the *h* in *his, him,* and *her* when it follows another word.
>
> He gets in ꞯis car.
> She didn't know ꞯim.
> She locked ꞯer car door.

CD 3; Track 9

A His / Him / Her Listen and repeat the sentences. Listen for the linking in each sentence.

1. He gets in ꞯis car.
2. He gets out of ꞯis car.
3. These two guys jump in ꞯis car.
4. They almost hit ꞯim.
5. She didn't know ꞯim.
6. She got in ꞯer car.
7. She locked ꞯer car door.
8. He showed ꞯer a five-dollar bill.
9. He tried to open ꞯer door.
10. They told ꞯer she was lucky

B Partner Practice Sit with a partner and practice saying these sentences. Do not pronounce the *h* in *his, him,* and *her*.

1. He did his homework.
2. I don't know his name.
3. I think his name is Brian.
4. I wrote him a letter.
5. We called her yesterday.
6. She likes her job.
7. He forgot his keys.
8. I gave him twenty dollars.
9. I spoke to her about it.
10. I need his telephone number.

LISTENING 3: A DESCRIPTION

CD 3; Track 10

A **Listen and Circle**   Listen to this description of the carjacker. Which person matches the description?

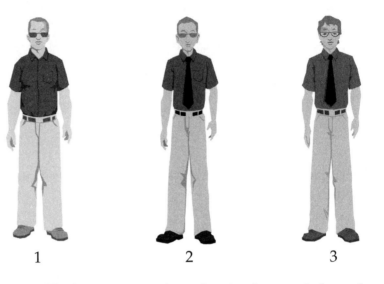

1   2   3

CD 3; Track 10

B **Write Key Words**   Listen again and write the words from the description that helped you choose the carjacker in Exercise A.

_____   _____

_____   _____

_____   _____

_____   _____

C **Answer the Questions**   How did the woman answer each question? Use your notes from Exercise A to write your answers.

1. Can you describe him?

_____

_____

2. Think about his face. Did he have a moustache . . . a beard?

_____

3. Gold? Silver?

_____

4. How about glasses? Was he wearing sunglasses?

_____

5. Do you remember anything about his clothes?

_____

SPEAKING

Ⓐ Tell the Story   This woman was the victim of a carjacking. Sit with another student, look at the pictures and tell the story of what happened to her. Practice your story so that you can easily tell it to another student. Then, change partners and compare your stories.

B Discuss   Sit in a small group and read each situation. Discuss what to do in each situation.

1. You are getting into your car. A man comes up behind you and says, "Give me your car keys."

2. You just came out of a shopping mall late at night. Your car is in a large parking lot, but the parking lot is almost empty. As you come near your car, you see a man walking toward you.

3. You are driving your car on a quiet street. The car in front of you stops suddenly and you stop just in back of it. The two people in the car get out and start to move toward your car.

4. You are in your car and you are stopped at a stop sign. Your doors are locked, but your window is part way down. A person comes up to your window and says, "I'm looking for the post office. Can you give me directions?"

C Write   Sit with another student. Write five suggestions to keep yourself and your car safe from a theft or from a carjacking. Share your list with the class.

1. **Always lock your car doors.** _____

2. _____

3. _____

4. _____

5. _____

INTERNET ACTIVITY

A Search for Information   Enter "prevent carjackings" into your computer Search Engine. List three more ideas for preventing a carjacking.

_____

_____

_____

YOU'RE FIRED

BEFORE YOU LISTEN

A List   Look at the picture above. This employee has just been fired. Sit with a partner. List five common reasons that people are fired from their jobs.

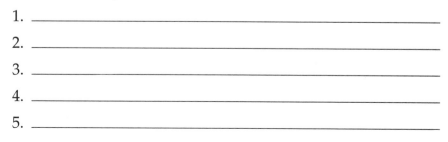

1. _____
2. _____
3. _____
4. _____
5. _____

LISTENING 1: PERSON ON THE STREET

Interview Question:

- *Did anyone at your job ever get fired?*

Listening Note: Predicting

When you listen, it helps to have an idea in mind. As you listen, you can compare your ideas about what will happen with the ideas of the speaker.

A Predict   Look at the photos below. On the first line, write your prediction. Guess the reason that each person was fired.

B Listen for Information   Listen to each interview. Then, write the reason the person got fired. Was your prediction correct?

CD 3; Track 11

1. My prediction: _____

   _____

   Reason: _____

   _____

2. My prediction: _____

   _____

   Reason: _____

   _____

3. My prediction: _____

   _____

   Reason: _____

   _____

VOCABULARY

A **Key Words**   Discuss the new vocabulary. Then, complete the sentences.

dental hygienist	a person who works in a dental office; Duties include cleaning teeth and taking x-rays
evaluation	a written opinion by the boss about your work
personal	private
schedule	a person's work days and hours
to complain	to say that you are not happy or not satisfied with something
to call in sick	to call work and say you cannot work that day because you are sick
to depend on	to have confidence or trust in someone or something

1. The boss gives each employee an _____ twice a year.

2. You cannot make _____ phone calls at work.

3. The boss can always _____ his workers to do their jobs well.

4. The employee _____ because she had a fever.

5. The _____ cleaned my teeth.

6. If customers begin to _____ about an employee, the boss will watch the employee carefully.

7. I don't like my _____ because I have to work every weekend.

B **Apply the Vocabulary**   Complete the sentences with your own responses.

1. People often complain about _____ and _____.

2. People call in sick when _____.

3. If I need a ride to school or to work, I can depend on _____.

4. I never talk about personal problems with _____.

5. The employee received a poor evaluation because he _____.

6. What work schedule would you like? _____

LISTENING 2: THE DENTIST AND THE DENTAL HYGIENIST

Ⓐ Listen for Reasons Doctor Park is a dentist. Shelly, a dental hygienist, works in his office. Doctor Park fired Shelly today. Listen to each person explain the situation. List three reasons Dr. Park fired Shelly. You do not need to write complete sentences.

1. _____

2. _____

3. _____

Listening Note: Listening for opinions
When you listen to two people speak about the same event, each person will have his or her own opinion and feelings about the event.

Ⓑ Listen for Opinions Read each statement about work. Then, listen to the two speakers again. Is the sentence expressing Dr. Park's opinion or Shelly's opinion? Compare your answers with a partner.

	Dr. Park	Shelly
1. Leave your problems at home.	____	____
2. It's okay to call in sick once or twice a month.	____	____
3. If a family member is sick, you might need to change your work schedule.	____	____
4. It's okay to talk about your personal problems at work.	____	____
5. If you do your job well, the boss shouldn't fire you.	____	____
6. Calling in sick once or twice a month is not acceptable.	____	____
7. It's okay to leave work early if you have a good reason.	____	____
8. The patients are our friends.	____	____

Ⓒ Share Your Opinion What is your opinion about Doctor Park firing Shelly? Do you think he was right to fire her? Why or why not? Discuss your opinion with the class.

Listening Note: True-False statements

Sometimes a true-false statement has two parts. If both parts of the statement are true, the statement is true. If one part of the statement is false, the entire statement is false.

D True or False   Read each statement. If the statement is *true*, circle T. If the statement is *false*, circle F.

1. When Shelly needed to take her mother to the doctor, she called in sick.   T   F

2. Shelly sometimes left work early so she could spend time with her boyfriend.   T   F

3. Many of Shelly's patients were unhappy with her, so they complained to the dentist.   T   F

4. While she cleaned the patient's teeth, Shelly told them about her personal life.   T   F

5. Shelly is upset because she saw her boyfriend with another woman.   T   F

6. When the dentist gave Shelly her evaluation, he fired her.   T   F

7. The dentist fired Shelly because she was not a good hygienist.   T   F

8. The dentist couldn't depend on Shelly, so he fired her.   T   F

E Complete the Sentences   Use the information you have learned to complete the statements about Shelly.

1. Shelly sometimes left early because _____.

2. Shelly didn't want to work on Saturday because _____.

3. The patient was crying because _____.

4. The other dental hygienist complained about Shelly because _____.

5. The dentist fired Shelly because _____.

STRUCTURE

🎧 **A Dictation**   Listen and write the sentences you hear.

CD 3; Track 13

1. _____
2. _____
3. _____
4. _____
5. _____
6. _____

▶ **Grammar Note: Past continuous tense**

The past continuous tells about an action that was in progress at a time in the past.

She was cleaning a patient's teeth.
She was always talking about her problems.

B Past Continuous Tense   Use a verb from the box and complete the sentences with the past continuous tense. Some words may be used more than once.

| tell | shop | see | bring | take |
| clean | have | cry | leave | |

1. Shelly ___**was having**___ problems with her boyfriend.

2. Shelly's boyfriend _____ another woman.

3. One day when Shelly _____ at the mall, she saw her boyfriend with another woman.

4. Shelly _____ always _____ her patients about her problems.

5. Shelly _____ always _____ her personal problems to work.

6. When Dr. Park walked into the examining room, Shelly and her patient _____.

7. The hygienist _____ an x-ray of a patient's teeth.

8. The hygienist _____ a patient's teeth.

9. Shelly _____ work early once a week and the other hygienist _____ her patients.

PRONUNCIATION

Pronunciation Note: Linking

Linking means joining or saying together. Link the final consonant of a word with the beginning vowel in the next word.

comes in late

three times a month

work on Saturday

A Listen and Repeat   Listen and repeat these short phrases and sentences.

1. come in late

2. call in sick

3. three times a month

4. work overtime

5. depend on

6. problems at home

7. I'm a dentist.

8. She's a good hygienist.

9. Take one day off a week.

10. My patients are happy.

B Partner Practice   Sit with a partner and practice saying these sentences. Try to link the sounds.

1. I'm a student.

2. I go to school _____ days a week.

3. I never come in late.

4. We don't have class on Sunday.

5. I work all day.

6. You can depend on me.

7. What's up?

8. How's everything?

9. Have a nice weekend.

10. That's all!

LISTENING 3: CALLING IN SICK

Ⓐ Write Sit with a partner. Write six reasons that people call in sick to work. Give four acceptable reasons and two unacceptable reasons.

Acceptable reasons to call in sick to work:

1. _____

2. _____

3. _____

4. _____

Unacceptable reasons to call in sick to work:

1. _____

2. _____

Listening Note: This is _____(name)_____.
When you speak on the phone, the correct form for saying your name is *This is ____(name)____*.

Ⓑ Write the Reason Listen to each conversation. Each worker is calling in sick. What reason does the worker give? Write the reason. When you finish, decide which reasons are acceptable. Which reasons are unacceptable?

CD 3; Track 15

Call 1: _____

Call 2: _____

Call 3: _____

Call 4: _____

Ⓒ Identify the Speakers In each call, an employee is speaking to a person at work. Listen to each call again and write the position or job of each person.

CD 3; Track 15

<u>Call 1</u>

MR. BARKER: __boss_____

JIM: _____

<u>Call 2</u>

CINDY WATERS: _____

ANN: _____

MR. COOPER: _____

Call 3

        SAM GARCIA: _____

       MATT BROWN: _____

Call 4

        LEAH MASON: _____

        CELIA HONG: _____

       MRS. DAVIS: _____

SPEAKING

Ⓐ Discuss and Decide   Sit in a group and discuss each situation. As a boss, which employees would you keep? Which employees would you fire?

1. The employee comes in late once a week.

2. The employee is unfriendly to the other workers.

3. The employee makes a lot of mistakes on customer orders.

4. The employee works at a cash register. Several times a week, a small amount of money is missing from the cash register drawer.

5. The employee fell at home and has a broken leg. This person cannot work for three months.

6. The employee is hard-working and efficient. But, he has a child who is often sick. He misses two or three days of work a month.

Ⓑ Complete and Share   Complete this information about your job or the job of someone you know. Share your information with your group. Talk about sick day policies and other policies that the company has. Ask and answer questions in your discussion.

1. I work at _____.

2. I work _____ days a week, from _____ to _____ (hours).

3. I am (often/seldom/never) late for work.

4. If I'm going to be late for work, I have to _____.

5. If an employee is often late for work, _____.

6. I have _____ sick days.

   I have _____ personal days.

   I have _____ vacation days.

7. When I need a sick day, I have to _____

   _____.

8. So far this year, I have taken _____ sick days.

9. I took a sick day in _____ (month) because _____

   _____.

C **Write a Dialogue** Sit with a partner and write a dialogue. One of you is an employee and one of you is the boss or the office manager. The employee is calling in sick to work. Practice your dialogue. Then, present it to the class.

THE TITANIC

BEFORE YOU LISTEN

A **Read**   Read the information about icebergs. Underline and discuss any new vocabulary.

Icebergs

Icebergs are pieces of snow and ice that break off from glaciers or from the ice shelf in Greenland or Antarctica. Some icebergs are very small, but others are the size of a house or a tall building. Icebergs come in many shapes; they can be flat, tall, pointed, or have a round top. As an  iceberg floats in the open water, it breaks into smaller pieces and melts slowly. It often takes many months for an iceberg to melt. Icebergs in the North Atlantic Ocean present a danger to ships. The International Ice Patrol flies over the North Atlantic Ocean and provides information to ships on the location of icebergs. Also, ships use radar and satellites to check for icebergs.

B **True or False** Read the sentences. Circle *T* if the statement is *true* or *F* if the statement is *false*.

1. An iceberg can be larger than a house.   T   F

2. When an iceberg gets to open water, it begins   T   F
   to melt.

3. After an iceberg breaks off from a glacier, it   T   F
   melts in a few days.

4. An iceberg can look like a mountain in the water.   T   F

5. Ships have many ways to check for the location   T   F
   of icebergs.

C **Label a Map** Before you listen, look at this map of the world. A continent is a large land mass. Talk with a partner and label the continents.

LISTENING 1: PERSON ON THE STREET

Interview question:

- *How many continents are there?*

CD 3; Track 16

A Listen and Complete   Each speaker is talking about the continents. Listen and complete the information.

1. According to this speaker, there are _____ continents.

   They are _____

   _____ .

2. According to this speaker, there are _____ continents.

   They are _____

   _____ .

3. According to this speaker, there are _____ continents.

   They are _____

   _____ .

B Discuss   Your view of the world and the continents depends on the country you are from. What did you learn in school? How many continents are there?

C Using the Map   Write the names of the oceans on the map: Pacific, Atlantic, Indian, Arctic, Southern. The Titanic was crossing the Atlantic Ocean. Which part of the ocean might have icebergs?

VOCABULARY

Ⓐ Key Words   Discuss the new vocabulary words. Then, complete the sentences below.

millionaire	a rich person who has more than a million dollars
on board/aboard	on a ship
luxury	very comfortable and expensive
to approach	to come near
crewman	a person who works on a ship
to rip	to tear, make a hole in
to sink	to slowly fall to the bottom of a body of water
lifeboats	small open boats on a large ship, used in an emergency
disaster	a terrible event, often with the loss of many lives

1. The ship _____ to the bottom of the ocean.

2. There were over two thousand people _____ the ship.

3. The first and only voyage of the Titanic ended in _____.

4. The iceberg _____ a large hole in the side of the ship.

5. There was no radar in the early 1900s. A _____ stood on the deck and watched for icebergs or other dangers.

6. A _____ has enough money to buy a beautiful home.

7. The ship did not have enough _____ for all the passengers.

8. No one knew that the ship was _____ icebergs.

9. The _____ ship had dining rooms, a swimming pool, and libraries.

LISTENING 2: THE TITANIC DISASTER

CD 3; Track 17

A **Listen for Information**   Listen to this story about the voyage of the Titanic. Who was Arthur Ryerson? What happened to him? After you listen, tell the class any other information you remember about the disaster.

CD 3; Track 17

B **Note-Taking**   Listen to the story again. Complete this information about the disaster.

1. Where did the Titanic leave from? _____

2. Where was it traveling? _____

3. When did the Titanic leave England? _____

4. How many people were on board? _____

5. What was the date of the accident? _____

6. How large was the hole? _____

7. How many people lost their lives? _____

C **Map Skills**   Look back at the map of the continents and the oceans on page 120. Where was the Titanic when it hit the iceberg?

> ## Listening Note: Sentence Sense
> When you hear a sentence, you often understand some of the words, but not all of them. Don't concentrate on single words. Think about the meaning of the whole sentence. What is the story about? What other words in the sentence can help you figure out the meaning?

CD 3; Track 18

D **Listen for Meaning**   Listen to these sentences from the beginning of the story. You may understand some of the words, but not all of them. Circle the correct meaning of the sentence.

1. a. Arthur Ryerson was going to take a trip on the Titanic.
   b. Arthur Ryerson was a famous person.

2. a. This was the first trip for the Titanic.
   b. The ship was going to England.

3. a. The ship had many things to do.
   b. The ship was filled with people.

4. a. The Titanic left England with many people.
   c. Arthur Ryerson knew many of the 2,224 people.

5. a. It was clear and cold.
   b. It was raining and cold.

6. a. A ship is a dangerous place to be.
   b. No one knew that the ship was near icebergs.

E Comprehension Questions   Read the questions and circle the correct answer.

1. Where was the ship traveling?
   a. from New York to England
   b. from England to New York
   c. around the world

2. How did Arthur Ryerson spend his first days on the ship?
   a. playing cards with his friends
   b. sleeping
   c. writing letters

3. What was the weather at the time of the accident?
   a. it was raining
   b. it was snowing
   c. it was clear

4. At what time did the ship hit the iceberg?
   a. in the morning
   b. in the evening
   c. at night

5. Who saw the iceberg first?
   a. one of the crewmen
   b. one of the passengers
   c. Arthur Ryerson

6. Where did the iceberg hit the Titanic?
   a. the left side
   b. the right side
   c. the back of the ship

7. Who got into the lifeboats first?
   a. the crew
   b. the first people to reach them
   c. the women and children

8. What did Arthur Ryerson do after the ship hit the iceberg?
   a. he continued to play cards
   b. he helped the women and children into the life boats
   c. he radioed for help

9. Why did so many people lose their lives?
   a. The water was cold.
   b. The ship caught on fire.
   c. There were not enough lifeboats.

STRUCTURE

> ### Grammar Note: Past Continuous
> The past continuous shows an action that was in progress at a time in the past.
>
> Arthur Ryerson **was sitting** in the smoking room.
> The passengers on the ship **were relaxing.**

CD 3; Track 19

Ⓐ Dictation   Listen and write the sentences you hear. In all the sentences, the verb is in the past continuous tense.

1. _____

2. _____

3. _____

4. _____

5. _____

6. _____

Ⓑ Past Continuous Tense   Answer each question about the Titanic disaster. Answer in a complete sentence. Use the past continuous tense in your answer.

1. Where was the ship going?

   _____

2. What was Arthur Ryerson doing when the ship hit the iceberg?

   _____

3. What were many of the passengers doing when the ship hit the iceberg?

   _____

4. What was the band doing when they heard the alarm?

   _____

5. What were women and children doing when the Titanic sank?

   _____

6. What was Arthur Ryerson doing when the ship sank?

   _____

PRONUNCIATION

CD 3; Track 20

Listening Note: of

We often do not hear the *f* in the word *of*.

the decks of the ship — the decks o*f* the ship

Before a vowel or an *h*, *f* sounds like *v*.

of April — ov April
three of his friends - three ov his friends

CD 3; Track 20

A Of   Listen carefully and complete these sentences.

1. The Titanic pulled _____ _____ port on April 10, 1912.

2. The first four _____ _____ the trip were clear and cold.

3. Arthur Ryerson was playing cards with several _____ _____ friends.

4. None _____ _____ knew of the danger ahead.

5. The evening _____ _____ 14 was relaxed.

6. He was in a smoking room with three _____ _____ friends.

7. _____ _____ the crewmen was standing watch.

8. There was no room for _____ _____ the men.

9. He returned to his _____ _____ cards.

10. It was _____ _____ the worst sea disasters in history.

B Partner Practice   Sit with a partner. Take turns saying these sentences.

1. I'd like a cup of coffee.

2. I drank a glass of juice.

3. Could I have a glass of water?

4. All of us came late.

5. I finished some of the homework, but not all of it.

6. She's one of the best students.

7. I don't have a lot of time.

LISTENING 3: A CRUISE

Ⓐ Before You Listen   You are going to hear a woman describe her cruise to Alaska. What are six questions that you would like to ask her? Write the questions below.

1. _____

2. _____

3. _____

4. _____

5. _____

6. _____

Ⓑ Note-Taking   Listen and complete the information about the cruise.

CD 3; Track 21

1. The cruise to Alaska left from _____.

2. The cruise was _____ days long.

3. The ship carried about _____ passengers.

4. Name two excursions that this woman took.

   _____

   _____

5. The weather was _____.

6. Name three activities for passengers onboard the ship.

   _____

   _____

   _____

7. Name two things that the passengers learned during the lifeboat practice.

   _____

   _____

8. This cruise probably cost about _____.

Ⓒ Review and Discuss   Look at your questions in Exercise A. Check the questions that the woman answered. Did the woman answer all of your questions? Would you enjoy this cruise?

SPEAKING

Ⓐ Order the Events   Sit with another student and put the events of the Titanic disaster in order from 1 to 7.

_____ Women and children got into the lifeboats.

_____ Radio operators immediately called for help.

__1__ The Titanic hit an iceberg.

_____ The Titanic sank in the icy waters.

_____ Another ship, the Carpathia, arrived two hours after the Titanic sank and began to pick up the survivors in the lifeboats.

_____ The Titanic broke in two.

_____ As people in the lifeboats watched, the Titanic sent up emergency rockets.

Ⓑ Read and Discuss   Read the following information about the Titanic disaster. Then, sit in a small group and answer the discussion questions on the next page.

- The radio operator on the Titanic received many reports of icebergs from other ships in the area. The radio operator thought that the captain knew of the iceberg warnings, so he did not deliver them.

- The Titanic was traveling at full speed in icy water.

- There was another ship in the area, the Californian. The radio operator of the Californian sent a warning to the Titanic that there were icebergs in the area. The radio operator on the Titanic replied, "Keep out! Shut up!" At 11:15, the radio operator on the Californian turned off his radio and went to bed.

- After midnight, the crew on the Californian saw rockets in the sky from a large ship just a few miles away. They told the captain, but he thought that the other ship was having a big party and so he did nothing.

- At the time, the law only required 16 lifeboats on a large ship. That is the number of lifeboats that the Titanic had on board.

- The captain and crew on the Titanic never had a lifeboat practice for an emergency. Some of the lifeboats, which could carry 65 people, only had 20 or 30 people in them.

- The Carpathia, a ship about 50 miles away, heard the S.O.S signal from the Titanic. It immediately headed at full speed to the rescue. The Titanic sank at 2:20, but the Carpathia was not able to reach the Titanic until 4:10. The Carpathia picked up the survivors in the lifeboats and headed to New York.

Discussion questions:

1. What information surprised you?

2. What mistakes were made on the evening of April 14, 1912?

3. The Carpathia arrived only two hours after the Titanic sank, but they found no survivors in the water. What was the reason for this?

4. Who was responsible for the disaster?

5. Did so many people need to die?

6. What laws do you think changed after the Titanic disaster?

C **Write a Conversation**   Sit with another student and write a conversation between a woman who survived the Titanic disaster and a government investigator. You can use the questions below to help you. Share your conversations with the class.

A: I'm a government representative and I am interviewing survivors of the terrible disaster. Do you think you could answer a few questions?

B: I'll try.

▶ **HELPFUL EXPRESSIONS**

Who were you traveling with?

Where was your room on the Titanic?

How was the weather on the night of April 14th?

Did you see any small icebergs in the water that day?

The ship hit the iceberg at 11:30. What were you doing at that time?

What orders did the captain give?

What time did you get into the lifeboat?

Did you ever have any emergency practices on the Titanic?

How many people were in your lifeboat?

What time did the Titanic fire its emergency rockets?

Could you see another ship in the distance?

How long were you in the lifeboat?

D **Interview** Interview a person who would like to take a vacation on a cruise ship.

1. Where do you want to travel?	
2. When do you want to go?	
3. Who will you travel with?	
4. Do you want to travel on a big ship or a small ship?	
5. How long do you want to travel?	
6. How much do you think the cruise will cost?	

INTERNET ACTIVITY

A **Search and Plan** Use a search engine to find the name of a major cruise line. Find a specific cruise and complete the following information. Sit in a small group and tell your classmates about your cruise plans.

I'm going to take a cruise on _____ (cruise line).

I'm going to travel to _____.

I'm planning to leave on _____.

The weather at that time of year is _____.

The cruise is _____ days.

We're going to leave from _____.

The ship stops at several ports, including _____

_____.

The ship is (large/small). It carries _____ passengers.

The cost of the cruise is _____.

DREAMS

BEFORE YOU LISTEN

A Discuss   Sit with a partner and talk about your dreams.

1. Did you dream last night?
2. Do you ever remember your dreams?
3. Do you ever dream about your childhood?
4. In your dreams, do you ever speak English?
5. Do you ever have nightmares (bad dreams)?

B Read and Discuss   Read the article about dreams. Underline and discuss any new vocabulary words.

Sleep

People spend almost one-third of their lives sleeping. The body needs seven to eight hours of sleep a night, but many people get only five or six hours.

There are two kinds of sleep, NREM sleep and REM sleep. NREM stands for Non-Rapid Eye Movement and REM stands for Rapid Eye Movement. NREM sleep is sometimes called "quiet sleep," a time when the body is resting. Blood pressure falls, the heart rate slows, and breathing is slow and regular. The body shows little activity and the eyes show little movement. The body and the mind are at rest. REM sleep is active sleep. Blood pressure, heart rate, and breathing are the same as when a person is awake. A person's eyes are moving rapidly under his or her eyelids.

People dream during both NREM and REM sleep. However, most dreams occur during REM sleep. These dreams are active, colorful, and often frightening. In fact, almost two-thirds of all dreams are unpleasant or scary. These dreams are called nightmares. For thousands of years, people have been trying to interpret dreams, that is, to find the meaning of dreams. No one can tell you exactly what a specific dream means, but it is still interesting to describe your dreams and try to figure out what they mean to you.

C Apply the Reading   Read each statement. Does it describe REM or NREM sleep? Write REM or NREM on the line.

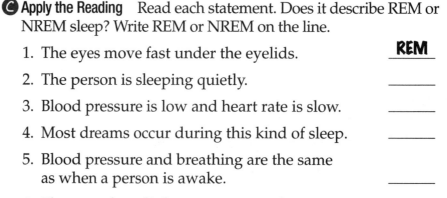

1. The eyes move fast under the eyelids.   **REM**

2. The person is sleeping quietly.   _____

3. Blood pressure is low and heart rate is slow.   _____

4. Most dreams occur during this kind of sleep.   _____

5. Blood pressure and breathing are the same as when a person is awake.   _____

6. The eyes show little movement under the eyelids.   _____

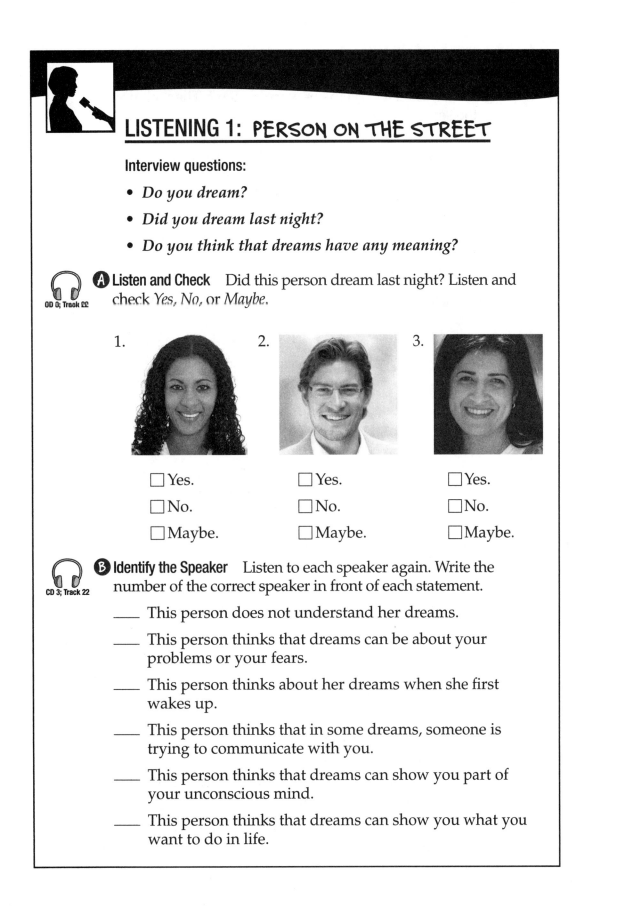

LISTENING 1: PERSON ON THE STREET

Interview questions:

- *Do you dream?*
- *Did you dream last night?*
- *Do you think that dreams have any meaning?*

A Listen and Check   Did this person dream last night? Listen and check *Yes, No,* or *Maybe.*

CD 3; Track 22

1.

☐ Yes.
☐ No.
☐ Maybe.

2.

☐ Yes.
☐ No.
☐ Maybe.

3.

☐ Yes.
☐ No.
☐ Maybe.

B Identify the Speaker   Listen to each speaker again. Write the number of the correct speaker in front of each statement.

CD 3; Track 22

_____ This person does not understand her dreams.

_____ This person thinks that dreams can be about your problems or your fears.

_____ This person thinks about her dreams when she first wakes up.

_____ This person thinks that in some dreams, someone is trying to communicate with you.

_____ This person thinks that dreams can show you part of your unconscious mind.

_____ This person thinks that dreams can show you what you want to do in life.

VOCABULARY

A Key Words Discuss the new vocabulary. Then, complete the sentences.

childhood	the time when a child is young, from birth to about age 13
psychologist	a doctor who studies the mind and behavior of people
fear	a strong feeling of fright or worry about a danger
to face (a problem)	to meet or take care of a problem
to solve	to find an answer or a solution to a problem
personality	a person's character; manner of acting
aggressive	unfriendly; violent
frightened	scared; afraid; very upset
shy	quiet; not comfortable with people, especially strangers
to stand for	to represent; be an example of something else
failure	not successful, a person who fails

1. I have a _____ of snakes.

2. They are seeing a _____ to talk about their family problems.

3. My brother has a friendly and outgoing _____.

4. In a dream, a queen might _____ a person's mother.

5. He's worried that the new business might be a _____.

6. My sister is quiet and _____ when she meets new people.

7. I lived in Mexico during my _____. I came to the United States when I was fifteen.

8. If we can't _____ our marriage problems, we should see a counselor.

9. My son is _____ of the dark, so we put a small light in his room.

10. Charles is _____ and gets into fights easily.

11. You can't run away from your problem, you have to _____ it.

B Use the Vocabulary   Use the new vocabulary and write the opposite of each word.

1. outgoing - _____
2. adulthood - _____
3. success - _____
4. run away from - _____
5. friendly, peaceful - _____
6. calm, relaxed - _____

LISTENING 2: DREAMS

CD 3; Track 23

A Listen and Discuss   Listen to this information about dreams. After you listen, discuss the questions.

1. What facts did you learn about dreams?
2. What do some psychologists believe about dreams?
3. We often dream in symbols. What might some of these symbols mean?

CD 3; Track 23

B Match   Listen to the information again. Match each symbol with an idea that it might represent.

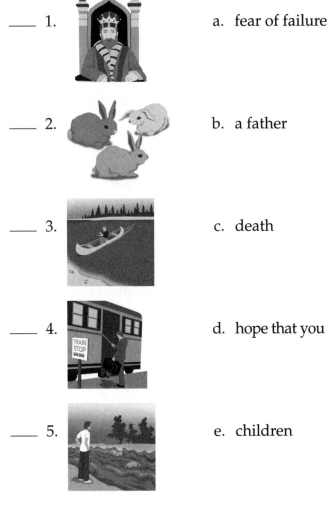

_____ 1.   a. fear of failure

_____ 2.   b. a father

_____ 3.   c. death

_____ 4.   d. hope that you will be successful

_____ 5.   e. children

C **True or False**   Read the statement below. Then, listen to the first part of this talk. Circle *T* if the statement is true, or *F* if the statement is false.

1. People usually have one or two dreams a week.   T   F

2. Most dreams are about 10 minutes long.   T   F

3. Dreams are in color.   T   F

4. Men are more aggressive than women in dreams.   T   F

5. Most dreams are happy or pleasant.   T   F

6. The most common dream is that someone or   T   F
    something is chasing you.

Listening Note: Fact vs. Opinion

A fact is information that is real. It is something that we can see or prove.

An opinion is an idea. For opinions, we use words like *think*, *believe*, and *might*.

Fact: People's eyes move when they are dreaming.
Opinion: Our dreams might represent our fears.

D **Fact or Opinion**   Read each statement about dreams. Write *Fact* or *Opinion* after each statement. Discuss your answers.

1. People dream four to six times a night.   _____

2. In dreams, we try to solve problems.   _____

3. If we dream about a king and queen, we
    are dreaming about our father and mother.   _____

4. Dreams can show us our future.   _____

5. Some dreams are short and other dreams
    are long.   _____

6. One common dream is of being in an accident. _____

7. A dream about a long trip means that we
    are worried about death.   _____

8. It is possible to have the same dream
    many times.   _____

Listening Note: but

But shows contrast. It completes the sentences with an idea that is the opposite or different from the first idea.

I often remember my dreams, *but* my sister doesn't remember hers.

REM sleep is usually active, *but* NREM sleep is usually quiet.

CD 3; Track 24

E Finish the Sentence   Listen to the first part of each sentence. Circle the second part of the sentence.

1. a. but other dreams are short.
   b. but other dreams are in color.

2. a. but women's dreams are aggressive, too.
   b. but women's dreams are more about friends and family.

3. a. but it was about losing a tooth.
   b. but I don't remember my dream.

4. a. but I forget them after I get up.
   b. but I sometimes have nightmares.

5. a. but I have the same dream over and over.
   b. but I don't understand them.

6. a. but he is 50 years old.
   b. but I never dream about my mother.

STRUCTURE

A Complete   Complete these sentences with your own responses.

1. Sometimes my dreams are happy, but _____

   _____.

2. My son sleeps peacefully all night, but my daughter _____

   _____.

3. I get up as soon as the alarm rings, but my husband _____

   _____.

4. My best friend has a lot of energy in the morning, but I ____

   _____.

5. I need seven or eight hours of sleep a night, but _____

   _____.

6. When I'm relaxed, I fall asleep easily, but when I'm under a lot of stress, _____

   _____.

> ### Grammar Note: Might
>
> *Might* shows probability or possibility.
>
> A dream **might continue** for an hour.
> You **might not remember** your dreams.

CD 3; Track 25

B Dictation   Listen and write the sentences you hear.

1. _____

2. _____

3. _____

4. _____

5. _____

6. _____

PRONUNCIATION

CD 3; Track 26

> ### Pronunciation Note: Word stress
>
> Stress can put special emphasis on any word or words in a sentence. Stress can change the meaning of the sentence.
>
> I **néver** dream.
> **Í** never dream.

CD 3; Track 26

A Word Stress   Listen carefully and mark the stressed word in each pair.

1. a. He snores all night.
   b. He snores all night.

2. a. You should go to bed earlier.
   b. You should go to bed earlier.

3. a. I want to hear about your dream.
   b. I want to hear about your dream.

4. a. What's the meaning of that dream?
   b. What's the meaning of that dream?

5. a. Dreams can be frightening.
   b. Dreams can be frightening.

6. a. I can't tell her my dream.
   b. I can't tell her my dream.

7. a. I never have nightmares.
   b. I never have nightmares.

B **Partner Practice** Sit with a partner. Say each sentence with special stress on one of the words. Your partner will point to the word that you stress.

1. I never remember my dreams.

2. I had the same dream!

3. What did you dream about?

4. I need an alarm clock to wake up.

5. I go to bed very late.

6. I have nightmares about my job.

7. I never dream about my job.

8. I don't get enough sleep.

9. My bed is too hard. I need a softer mattress.

LISTENING 3: TELL ME ABOUT YOUR DREAM

CD 3; Track 27

A **Match** Listen to six people describe their dreams. Match the dream with the correct picture.

_____   _____   _____

_____   _____   _____

ⓑ Listen and Circle   Listen to each dream again. Circle the letter of the correct sentence.

Dream 1. In this dream, the speaker
    a. is washing windows.
    b. is watching his father.
    c. is screaming.

Dream 2. This person
    a. is pregnant.
    b. wants to be pregnant.
    c. doesn't want to be pregnant.

Dream 3. This person
    a. had one long dream.
    b. dreamed the exact same dream three times.
    c. dreamed about the same situation three times.

Dream 4. In this dream, the person
    a. was running for exercise.
    b. was running away from an animal.
    c. was running away from her husband.

Dream 5. In this dream, the person
    a. finds a little money.
    b. finds a lot of money.
    c. steals some money.

Dream 6. In this dream, the children
    a. help the young woman.
    b. get in a boat.
    c. watch the woman go past.

ⓒ Listen and Interpret   Sit in a small group. Listen to the speakers again. Your group has three minutes to write one possible interpretation, or meaning, for each dream. Compare your ideas, then, continue with the next dream. One possible meaning is given for the first dream.

1. **He's worried about his father's health.**

2. _____

3. _____

4. _____

5. _____

6. _____

SPEAKING

A Interview   Interview a classmate about his or her sleeping habits.

1. What time do you go to bed?	
2. What time do you get up?	
3. Are you tired when you wake up?	
4. Do you need an alarm clock to wake you up?	
5. Is it easy for you to fall asleep?	
6. Do you read before you go to sleep?	
7. Do you watch TV before you go to bed?	
8. Do you take a hot bath before you go to sleep?	
9. Do you wake up during the night?	
10. Do you snore?	
11. Are you a heavy or a light sleeper?	

B Write   Work with a partner. Write five suggestions for getting a good night's sleep. Two have been written for you.

1. **Do not drink coffee before you go to bed.**
2. **Go to bed at about the same time every night.**
3. _____
4. _____
5. _____
6. _____
7. _____

C Interpret the Meaning Sit in a small group of three or four students. Decide on a possible meaning for each of the dream symbols below. Use your imagination. Under each picture, write two things it might stand for. Share your ideas with the other groups.

> **HELPFUL EXPRESSIONS**
>
> It might stand for a _____ .
> It might represent a _____ .
> It might be a symbol of/for _____ .
> It might mean that _____ .

_____   _____

_____   _____

_____   _____

_____   _____

D Partner Practice Work with a partner. Tell your partner about one of your dreams. Try to remember as many details as possible. Your partner will try to interpret your dream. Then, switch roles and repeat the exercise.

CREDIT CARDS

BEFORE YOU LISTEN

FIRST NATIONAL CREDIT COMPANY	CREDIT CARD STATEMENT	NAME Larry Williams 36 Davis Road Chicago, Illinois

ACCOUNT NUMBER	STATEMENT DATE	PAYMENT DUE DATE
2222-222-222	09-18	10-10

CREDIT LIMIT	CREDIT AVAILABLE	MINIMUM PAYMENT DUE
$2000.00	$1719.65	$40.00

REFERENCE NUMBER	SOLD	POSTED	ACTIVITY	AMOUNT
44411444		9-04	PAYMENT - THANK YOU	-$100.00
11331133	9-20	9-21	Best Shoes	$40.00
22112211	10-02	10-04	Elan Electronics	$120.00

Previous Balance	(+)	210.00		Current Amount Due	280.35
Purchases	(+)	160.50		Amount Past Due	
Payments	(-)	100.00		Amount Over Credit Line	
Credits	(-)			Minimum Payment Due	40.00
Finance Charge	(+)	9.85			
Late Fee	(+)	0.00			
NEW BALANCE	(=)	280.35		Interest Rate	19.80%

Ⓐ Complete the Information Look at the credit card statement and complete the information.

1. Larry's previous balance was $_____.

2. Last month he paid $_____ on his credit card.

3. This month, Larry charged $_____ on his credit card.

4. His finance charge is $_____.

5. His new balance is $_____.

6. Larry (paid/ didn't pay) a late fee last month.

7. The minimum payment due is $_____.

8. The interest rate on this card is _____ percent.

9. Larry must send in his payment by _____.

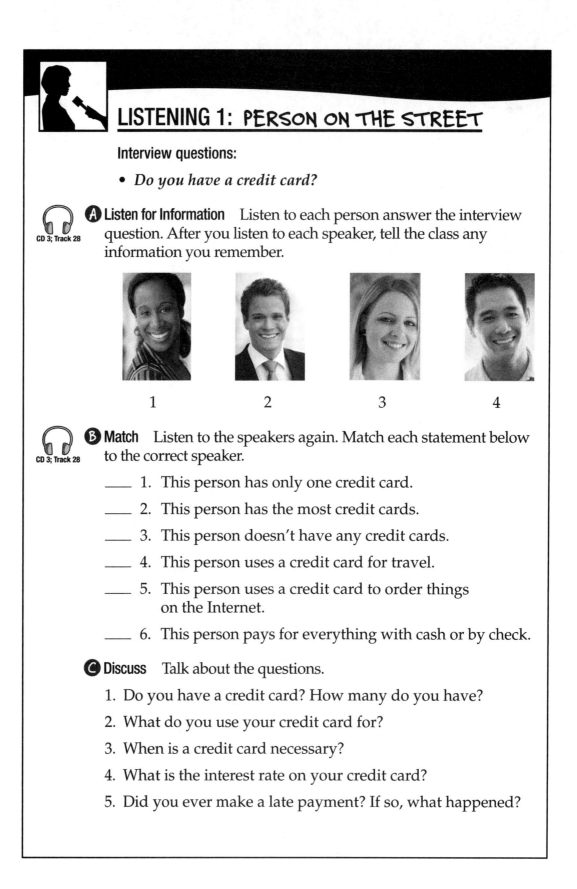

LISTENING 1: PERSON ON THE STREET

Interview questions:

- *Do you have a credit card?*

A Listen for Information   Listen to each person answer the interview question. After you listen to each speaker, tell the class any information you remember.

CD 3; Track 28

1   2   3   4

B Match   Listen to the speakers again. Match each statement below to the correct speaker.

CD 3; Track 28

_____ 1. This person has only one credit card.

_____ 2. This person has the most credit cards.

_____ 3. This person doesn't have any credit cards.

_____ 4. This person uses a credit card for travel.

_____ 5. This person uses a credit card to order things on the Internet.

_____ 6. This person pays for everything with cash or by check.

C Discuss   Talk about the questions.

1. Do you have a credit card? How many do you have?

2. What do you use your credit card for?

3. When is a credit card necessary?

4. What is the interest rate on your credit card?

5. Did you ever make a late payment? If so, what happened?

VOCABULARY

Ⓐ Key Words Discuss the new vocabulary. Then, complete the sentences.

to owe	to need to pay money to someone
to pay off	to pay all the money you owe
limit	the greatest amount allowed
receipt	a piece of paper that shows you paid a bill
mistake	something that is wrong or incorrect
balance	an amount of money that you have or that you owe
to raise	to increase
to loan	to give someone money that he will pay back later

1. I borrowed $1,000 and made a payment of $600. My _____ is now $400.

2. After I paid for my jacket, the clerk gave me a _____.

3. The interest rate on my credit card used to be 15 percent. Then, the bank _____ the rate to 22 percent.

4. I called my credit card company because they made a _____ on my bill.

5. I have a _____ of $5,000 on my credit card. I can't charge more than that amount.

6. When I bought my car, the bank _____ me $8,000.

7. Last year, I had a balance of $3,000 on my credit card bill. I finally _____ the total amount, so now I don't _____ anything.

Ⓑ Apply the Vocabulary Read the sentences and circle the correct answer.

1. If you don't make the minimum payment, the bank will charge you _____.
   a. a late fee   b. an interest rate

2. If you don't pay your bill on time, the credit card company can raise the _____.
   a. balance   b. interest rate

3. If your credit card limit is $5,000, you can charge _____.
   a. more than $5,000   b. $5,000 or less.

4. Every month, check your credit card statement with your _____.
   a. receipts   b. mistakes

LISTENING 2: RADIO TALK SHOW

 Listening Note: Numbers

Most students need a lot of practice with numbers. It takes a long time to feel comfortable with numbers in English.

CD 3; Track 29

A Complete the Information   You are listening to a radio talk show on credit cards. Callers are speaking to Jack Angeles, the president of Volo Credit Cards. The first caller is Mike. Listen to the first part of the call, *Understanding the Problem*, and complete the information. Compare your information with a partner. Then, listen again to check your information.

1. Mike bought a TV _____ ago.

2. He paid _____ for the TV.

3. Mike pays $_____ every month.

4. After one year, he still owes _____ on his credit card.

5. The interest rate on his card is _____ percent.

6. When Mike makes his monthly payment, most of the payment is for the _____.

CD 3; Track 30

B Note-Taking: Numbers   Jack Angeles is explaining the importance of paying more money on a credit card balance each month. Listen to the second part of the call, *Understanding Interest Rates*, and complete the chart below. You will need to listen two or more times.

Amount due on credit card: $5,000   Interest rate: 22%

Payment each month	Time to pay off card	Total amount of interest	Total cost of TV
$100		$_____	$_____
		$_____	$_____
		$_____	$_____

STRUCTURE

Ⓐ Complete the Sentences   Use the information from the chart on page 146 to complete the sentences.

1. If you pay $100 a month, __you will pay $8,700__ in interest.

2. If you pay $100 a month, __it will take you eleven years__ to pay for your TV.

3. If you pay $100 a month, your TV __will cost $_____.

4. If you pay $200 a month, _____ in interest.

5. If you pay $200 a month, _____ to pay for your TV.

6. If you pay $200 a month, your TV _____.

7. If you pay $300 a month, _____ in interest.

8. If you pay $300 a month, _____ to pay for your TV.

9. If you pay $300 a month, your TV _____.

Ⓑ Future Time Clauses   Complete the sentences about credit cards. Use the future tense. Answers will vary.

1. If you are late with a payment, _____

_____.

2. If you charge a lot of items on your credit card, _____

_____.

3. If you only pay the minimum each month, _____

_____.

4. If you can't make the payments on your credit card, _____

_____.

5. If you pay your balance every month, _____

_____.

PRONUNCIATION

CD 3; Track 31

> ## Pronunciation Note:
> ## More Practice with Linking
> Linking means joining or saying together. Link the final consonant of a word with the beginning vowel in the next word.
>
> rent a car
> two and a half years
> I bought a computer.
> I have a credit card.

CD 3; Track 31

A Linking   Listen and repeat these short phrases and sentences.

1. rent a car
2. a year and a half
3. make a payment
4. pay off
5. It's a call in show.
6. Mike is from Arizona.
7. You need a credit card to make a reservation.
8. You'll need about two years to pay off your card.

B Partner Practice   Sit with a partner and practice saying these sentences. Try to link the sounds.

1. I have a credit card.
2. I don't like to use it.
3. I only use it when I have to.
4. I bought a computer a few months ago.
5. It was about a thousand dollars.
6. I put it on my credit card.
7. I get a bill every month.
8. It's about ninety dollars a month.
9. I'll pay it off in a year.

LISTENING 3: CREDIT CARD PROBLEMS

 A Listen and Explain   Listen to the conversation between two friends. One friend is explaining her credit card problems. After you listen, talk with a partner. Explain the problem that this woman had with her credit card.

 Listening Note: Listening to a Story

When a person is speaking, you show your interest in the story by asking questions, by repeating information, and by making short comments, like *Oh, no! Really? Uh-oh. That's too bad.*

 B Listen for Responses   Listen to the conversation again. As you listen, write the missing responses.

CD 3; Track 32

A: I had a credit card. But now I don't. The credit card company took it away.

B: _____?

A: And it wasn't my fault.

B: _____.

A: I had a credit card. And I was good about not charging too much and paying it off every month. Then, last year, my sister wanted to use my card.

B: _____.

A: I didn't want to give it to her, but she needed to buy airline tickets to go on vacation and she didn't have the money. She promised to pay off the card.

B: _____.

A: Two thousand dollars.

B: _____!

A: When the first bill came, I gave it to her, but she didn't pay it. . . The company called me and called me.

B: _____?

A: They took away my credit card and now I have bad credit and I can't get a car loan.

B: _____.

SPEAKING

A Discuss   Sit in a small group and talk about credit cards.

1. Do you have a credit card? How many credit cards do you have? What is the interest rate? What do you charge? What do you pay for in cash?

2. Did you ever make a payment late? What happened?

3. Are you saving for something special? What are you planning to buy? When are you going to buy it? How are you going to pay for it?

4. When is it necessary to have a credit card?

5. Did you or anyone you know ever have a problem with a credit card? Explain the situation.

B Complete the Conversation   Sit with a partner and complete the conversation below. Person A is telling a story about a credit card problem. Write the responses for Person B. Then, practice the conversation with your partner. Show your interest in the story by asking questions, repeating information, or making short comments.

A: I owe so much money on my credit card.

B: _____

A: About $8,000.

B: _____

A: Well, for many years I had a credit card. And my limit was $500. Then, the company raised my credit limit to $1,000 and I had no problem. I always paid my balance in one or two months. I never spent more than $1,000, but they kept raising my limit. Soon it was $10,000.

B: _____

A: I was very careful and I never had a problem because I only charged a little. But then, one day, my son was playing soccer and he broke his leg. I don't have any medical insurance. He was only in the hospital for one day. But the bill for everything – doctors, hospital, x-rays . . was $10,000.

B: _____

A: That was two years ago and I still owe $8,000. It's going to take me years to pay off this card.

B: _____

C Complete and Share   Sit in a small group and read the following words of wisdom about money. In a small group, complete the next two sentences and think of two more examples. Share your ideas with your class.

What Money Can Buy

Money can buy a house, but not a home.
Money can buy a bed, but not sleep.
Money can buy a book, but not knowledge.
Money can buy a clock, but not time.
Money can buy medicine, but not health.
Money can buy make-up, but not _____.
Money can buy insurance, but not _____.
Money can buy _____, but not _____.
Money can buy _____, but not _____.

INTERNET ACTIVITY

A Calculate the Interest   On your search engine, look up *credit card interest calculator*. Enter an amount you want to borrow and the interest on a typical credit card. Complete the chart to show how much you will pay for the item for each payment amount.

Amount: $_____   Interest rate: _____%

Payment each month	Time to pay off card	Total amount of interest	Total cost
$100 _____	_____	$_____	$_____
$200 _____	_____	$_____	$_____
$300 _____	_____	$_____	$_____

"God bless mommy, daddy, spot and that Porsche I bought off the Internet with daddy's credit card."

CITY POPULATIONS

B Population Map

STUDENT A: Turn to page 43.

STUDENT B: Student A will look at the map on page 43 and ask about the population of these major cities. Look at the chart below and state the population.

Cities	Population
Seattle	594,000
San Francisco	765,000
Los Angeles	3,834,000
Las Vegas	559,000
Memphis	675,000
Houston	2,208,000
Chicago	2,837,000
Detroit	917,000
Miami	410,000
Washington, D.C.	588,000
Philadelphia	1,450,000
New York City	8,275,000
Boston	600,000

AUDIOSCRIPTS

UNIT 1: Do You Like Your Job?

Listening 1: Person on the Street (Page 2)

Interview Questions: What do you do? Do you like your job? What do you like about your job?

Conversation 1

A: What do you do?
B: I'm a police officer.
A: Do you like your job?
B: Yeah, I do.
A: What do you like about it?
B: Let's see . . . Well, the work is interesting. There's something different everyday. And my benefits. I get great benefits, medical, dental, good vacation.

Conversation 2

A: What do you do?
B: I'm a manicurist. I work in a nail salon.
A: How do you like your job?
B: It's good.
A: What do you like about it?
B: Let me think . . . I really like my coworkers. We're all from the same country and we're really friendly. We talk and laugh. And my hours are good. I work from 10:00 a.m to 6 p.m.

Conversation 3

A: What do you do?
B: I'm an auto mechanic.
A: Do you like your job?
B: Sure, it's okay.
A: What do you like?
B: Hmm. What do I like? My salary is good. I've been here two years, and I keep getting raises. And, the service station sends us for new training. We learn how to work on all the new engines.

Listening 2: Do You Like Your Job? (Page 5)

Speaker 1: I'm a toll collector on the Turnpike. I've been working there for seven years and I really like the job. I stand or sit on a stool and take the tolls from drivers. There's always a line so I have to work fast. The work is interesting and I'm always busy. Drivers need change or they want to buy tokens. Sometimes they ask for

directions or want to know the weather conditions on the road ahead. I can recognize every make and model of car and I see some beautiful ones.

My hours are great, from 11:00 P.M. to 7 A.M., so I can work after I put the children in bed. If I want, there's lots of overtime, especially on the weekends. The pay is good and I have medical benefits for myself and my family. I feel lucky to have this job.

Speaker 2: I'm a toll collector on the Turnpike. I've been working there for a year and I really hate the job. The work is boring. I just stand in a small booth and collect fifty cents or a token. It's the same thing over and over for eight or nine hours. In the winter, I'm always cold, especially my fingers. In the summer I'm always hot because there's no air conditioning. Also, I hate the smell of car fumes. The smell of gas gives me a headache.

My hours are terrible, from 11:00 P.M. TO 7 A.M. I can't go out with my friends because I have to be home by 10:00 to get ready for work. My boss is never satisfied. He complains that I work too slowly. And there's no opportunity for promotion. I don't want to collect tolls for the next thirty years. It's time to look for a new job.

D. Tone of voice. You will hear ten sentences about work. Listen to each person's tone of voice to help you decide if the speaker is describing something he likes or doesn't like about the job.

1. My hours are terrible.
2. The work is interesting and I'm always busy.
3. My hours are great.
4. The work is boring.
5. My boss always complains about my work.
6. The pay is good.
7. There's no opportunity for promotion.
8. It's the same thing over and over.
9. If I want, I can work lots of overtime.
10. In the winter, I'm always cold. In the summer, I'm always hot.

Structure (Page 6)

B. Dictation Listen and write the sentences you hear.

1. They work from 11 P.M. to 7 A.M.
2. She likes her hours.
3. He doesn't like to work at night.

4. He hates the smell of car fumes.
5. In the winter, he's always cold.

Pronunciation (Page 7)

> **Pronunciation note:** *And, Or*
> *And* often sounds like *and*. *Or* often sounds like *or*.
> My hands and feet are cold.
> I can't see my family or friends.

A. And/Or. Listen carefully and complete the sentences with *and* or *or*.

1. I sit or stand.
2. I usually work on Saturday and Sunday.
3. I can recognize every make and model.
4. I have medical benefits for myself and my family.
5. It's the same thing over and over.
6. I work eight or nine hours a night.
7. In the winter, the work is cold and boring.
8. I'm going to quit and find a new job.

Listening 3: Guess the Job (Page 8)

Conversation 1

A: How's your new job?
B: I really like it . . . most of the time.
A: What do you mean, most of the time?
B: The job's great when it's warm and sunny. But, when it's wet or cold, people still expect their mail.
A: How are your hours?
B: For me, they're great. I'm a morning person. We start at 6:00, sorting the mail. I start delivering by 9:00 and I'm back at the post office by 2:00.

Conversation 2

A: I got a job at Global Tours.
B: Great! What do you do there?
A: I help people with their travel plans. I make airline and hotel reservations. And I'm learning all about cruises, you know, about the different cruise lines and ships.
B: How's your boss?
A: She's great. She's giving me more and more responsibility.
B: Sounds like you found a good job.

Conversation 3

A: How's work?
B: Good. I always work four or five tables, so I'm making good tips.
A: What's the most popular order?
B: That's easy . . . the lasagna, it's really good.
A: How are your coworkers?
B: Everybody is friendly and we all help each other when things get busy.

A: Do you get any benefits?
B: Are you kidding? We get no benefits at all. The only benefit is my dinner – it's anything I want to eat that night – free.

Unit 2: Hurricane!

Listening 1: Person on the Street (Page 12)

Interview Question: Imagine that a Category 3 hurricane is going to hit the area where you live. Would you evacuate?

Speaker 1: I would leave. Definitely. We have two little boys – one and three years old. My house is important, but my family is more important. I would evacuate a few days early when the traffic is not so heavy.

Speaker 2: I think a hurricane would be exciting. I wouldn't evacuate. I'd get together with some of my friends and we'd experience the hurricane. I'd like to see one for myself. I'd only leave for a Category 5 hurricane.

Speaker 3: I watched TV and saw those pictures of Katrina, when it hit New Orleans . . when was that? I think in 2005. More than a thousand people died. I'd pack my car and go and stay with a friend. I'd try to get at least 100 miles from here.

Listening 2: A News Report (Page 15)

We are watching Hurricane Bobby closely. It is now a Category 1 hurricane with winds of 80 miles an hour. The storm is moving slowly; the weather satellites show that it is moving about eight miles an hour. But, it's growing and becoming stronger every hour. We expect that Bobby will hit Florida on Friday, about 48 hours from now. There is a hurricane watch in effect. There is no order to evacuate at this time. Some people are evacuating and leaving their homes, but most people are staying.

Our reporter is Jeff Miller. Jeff is talking to Mr. Morales who lives in Tampa. Mr. Morales has decided to evacuate.

R: Reporter Jeff Miller
M: Mr. Morales

R: Mr. Morales, it looks like you are leaving your home.
M: Yes, we are. We're going - my wife, my kids, my mother, she's 85, and the dog. I'm not taking any chances. We're only five miles from the water here, so we're leaving.
R: There is no order to evacuate. You don't have to leave.
M: I don't care. We were here last year for a Category 2 hurricane and it was terrible . . . with trees down . . . flooding . . . the wind. Forget it. We're not going to stay.
R: Where are you going?

M: To my sister's house. She lives about 75 miles from here . . in Orlando. I want to leave early, before the roads are crazy. We're taking two cars. I'm waiting for my wife to get home, then, we're going. She's filling up the car with gas and she's stopping at the drugstore for a prescription. My mother has heart problems, so we need her medications.

R: What are you taking?

M: We're bringing our important papers, like insurance policies, [um] licenses, documents like that. We're taking our photos . . . and small electronic equipment, like cameras and the laptop. Everyone is taking clothes, too.

R: Are you putting plywood on your windows?

M: You know . . I tried to. I went to the store, but there's no more plywood anywhere. The kids and I are cleaning up the yard now, taking everything in the yard - the chairs, and garbage cans, the grill - and putting it in the garage.

R: Good luck.

M: Thanks.

Structure (Page 17)

A. Dictation   Listen and write the sentences you hear.

1. Mr. Morales is talking to a reporter.
2. The hurricane is moving slowly.
3. It's becoming stronger.
4. Some people are leaving their homes.
5. Most people are staying.
6. Everyone is watching the weather on TV.

Pronunciation (Page 18)

Pronunciation Note: *want to, need to, have to, has to, going to*

When people speak, they often reduce the sound of *to* after these verbs. You don't hear the *t*.

going to – *gonna*	We aren't *gonna* stay.
want to – *wanna*	I *wanna* leave early.
need to – *needa*	We *needa* clean up the yard.
has to – *hasta*	She *hasta* get some gas.
have to – *haveta*	You don't *haveta* evacuate.

Note: When writing, always write *to*: need *to*

A. Listen and Complete.   Listen to each sentence and complete with the verb you hear.

1. I want to leave early.
2. We are going to leave soon.
3. She has to pick up the medication.
4. The hurricane is going to hit Florida.
5. We don't have to evacuate.
6. We need to clean up our yard.
7. We want to go before the roads are crazy.
8. My wife has to stop at the drugstore.
9. We need to get some extra cash.
10. We are going to take two cars.

Listening 3: A Radio Bulletin (Page 19)

1. Hurricane Watch

The National Weather Service has issued a hurricane watch for western Florida, along the Gulf coast. Hurricane Ann is 100 miles west of Florida, moving at seven miles an hour. It is a Category 1 hurricane. Residents are urged to prepare for the storm, clean their yards, and buy extra food and water. It is important to have a battery-operated radio.

2. Hurricane Warning

The National Weather Service has issued a hurricane warning for western Florida, along the Gulf Coast. Hurricane Ann is growing stronger and is now a Category 3 hurricane. It is 80 miles from Sarasota, moving at ten miles per hour. It will hit the coast tonight, about 6:00 P.M. The governor has issued an evacuation order for Sarasota County. All residents of Sarasota County who live within ten miles of the coast must prepare to evacuate their homes immediately. All schools and businesses in Sarasota will be closed tomorrow.

Unit 3: Diabetes

Listening 1: Person on the Street (Page 25)

Interview Question: What do you know about diabetes?

Speaker 1: Yeah, I know a little about diabetes. What do I know about diabetes? Just that you have to have a very restricted diet. And you have to check your blood sugar.

Speaker 2: Not much. It has something to do with your ability or your inability to produce insulin. And it has an effect on blood sugar levels.

Speaker 3: Well, I know that if you have diabetes, you have trouble with insulin. 'N, I think, that it's the insulin that helps your body use glucose. It's something like that, but I'm not really sure. But I do know that if you have too much glucose in your body, you can have all kinds of health problems.

Speaker 4: Well, I have a, have a, friend with diabetes. She has a . . . a little meter and she checks her blood sugar, I think, four times a day. And I know she's careful about her diet. But I really don't know much about it, about diabetes.

Listening 2: Could You Have Diabetes? (Page 27)

Could you or someone in your family have diabetes? Today, more than one in ten people in the United States have diabetes. Many people have diabetes, but they do not know it.

Who will get diabetes? Ask yourself these questions. First, does someone in your family have diabetes? Second, are you African-American, Hispanic, or Asian? If so, you have a greater possibility of diabetes. Third, do you know your blood pressure? People with high blood pressure are more likely to get diabetes. Next, are you heavy? Heavy people are more likely to get diabetes. Next, how old are you? In the past, most people with diabetes were older, usually over 60. But, today, many younger people have diabetes because they are heavy. And finally, do you exercise? People who do not exercise are more likely to get diabetes.

What are some of the signs, or symptoms, of diabetes? With diabetes, you usually don't feel sick. So, tell your doctor if you have any of these symptoms. Are you thirsty all the time? Do you often feel hungry, or want to eat more? Do you often feel tired? Do you need to go to the bathroom often, especially at night? Are you heavier every year? Are you having trouble with your eyes? If the doctor thinks you have diabetes you will need a simple blood test. If your glucose level is high, it shows that you have pre-diabetes or diabetes.

There is no cure for diabetes. If you have diabetes, the doctor will help you develop a health plan. The health plan usually has five parts. First, eat well. You can eat a regular healthy diet with lots of fruit, vegetables, low-fat dairy products, meat, and fish. If you are heavy, it is very important to lose weight. Second, exercise. Exercise every day for thirty to sixty minutes. Walking is great exercise. Third, take your medication, if it is necessary. Many people with diabetes do not need to take medication if they have a good diet and they exercise. But other people must take medication every day. Next, check your glucose level. Some people only need to check their glucose level once or twice a year. But, some people with diabetes need to check their level many times a day. Finally, learn everything you can about diabetes. Read books. Look on the Internet. Talk to other people with diabetes. Learn how to take good care of yourself.

Structure (Page 28)

A. Dictation   Listen and write the sentences you hear.

1. Do you have diabetes?
2. Does someone in your family have diabetes?
3. Do you know your blood pressure?
4. Are you over 60?
5. Are you having trouble with your eyes?
6. Do you exercise?

Pronunciation (Page 29)

Pronunciation note: Syllables

Words in English have one or more syllables. Listen to the vowels and the rhythm to help you hear the number of syllables.

One syllable	Two syllables	Three syllables	Four syllables
plan	doctor	exercise	medication
check	today	important	especially

A. Syllables.   Listen to these words. Write the number of syllables you hear.

1. sign ____
2. Internet ____
3. finally ____
4. symptoms ____
5. because ____
6. cure ____
7. problem ____
8. develop ____
9. diabetes ____
10. hungry ____
11. health ____
12. blood ____
13. necessary ____
14. diet ____
15. regular ____

Pronunciation note: Word Accent

In each word of two or more syllables, one syllable is accented. We say that syllable longer and louder than the other syllable(s). We put an accent mark on that syllable.

Two syllables	Three syllables	Four syllables
doctor	exercise	medication
today	important	especially

B. Word Accent.   Listen to the words. Put an accent mark on the accented syllable.

1. peo ple
2. In ter net
3. fi nal ly
4. symp toms
5. be cause
6. in su lin
7. prob lem
8. de vel op
9. di a be tes
10. hun gry
11. me ter
12. care ful
13. nec es sar y
14. di et
15. reg u lar

Listening 3: An Interview (Page 30)

David, thank you for talking to me about this topic. I know you have diabetes and that you use a meter. Can you tell me more about the meter you use and what it shows?

I have a meter – a blood sugar meter. I check my blood sugar four times a day and the meter tells what my blood sugar is. And I know from the number it gives whether it's too high or too low or it's ok. I get a little drop of blood from my finger. Then, I put that little spot of blood on a special piece of paper and that goes into the meter and I wait a few seconds and the meter gives me the number. And from that I know, like I said, if it's just right or too high or too low.

What is a normal blood sugar reading and what would a high reading be?

I check my blood sugar in the morning, before breakfast, and I also check it a few hours after every meal, so I check it a few hours after breakfast, a few hours after lunch, and a few hours after dinner. The reading should be between 80 and about 130, for me, that's normal. Below 65 is too low and I don't want it to be over 140.

What are you supposed to do if you're too high and what are you supposed to do if you're too low?

If it's too low, that's easy. I just need some sugar, I can eat almost anything, so I eat a bar of candy or drink a glass of orange juice, anything with a bit of sugar to raise the sugar level. If it's high, I can do some exercise, I can go out and take a walk or ride a bike, if the weather is OK. If the weather is bad, I try to do some exercises. I need some exercise because it lowers blood sugar.

I know you are very careful of your diet. What can you eat and what can't you eat?

My diet is really good, I like fruits and vegetables, so I eat lots of them.

What can't I eat? . . . .Well, traditionally, it was sugar. They always said, with diabetes, don't eat sugar. Don't eat sugar. Well, that's true. You have to be careful of sugar.

But it's the carbohydrates that are the real problem. The worst things are pasta, like . . . spaghetti, macaroni, things like that, and rice . . . especially white rice. And anything made with white flour is bad for you. That kind of carbohydrate raises the blood sugar very, very much. For me, if it's white, I don't eat it.

David, any final thoughts?

For me, I inherited diabetes and I've had it for a long time.

But, for most people, most people have diabetes from their lifestyle. They're heavy or they're eating the wrong things – a lot of fat, a lot of carbohydrates, a lot of sugar. Now, they are finding more and more children with diabetes. Kids today are watching TV more and playing on the computer. We need to help children to change their eating habits and to play outside more.

Unit 4: The Changing Face of the United States

Listening 1: Person on the Street (Page 35)

Interview Question: These charts show the population of the United States in 2000 and the projected population in 2050. Are you surprised by any of the information?

Speaker 1: Hmm. The Hispanic population is doubling. And the African-American population is remaining about the same. I'm surprised at the Asian population. Because that includes a lot of countries . . . China, Japan, Korea, India, Vietnam. I thought it was higher. It's going to double . . from 4% to 8%, but it's still not high.

Speaker 2: To me, this is all about the birth rate. White families are not having as many children. The African-American population is staying about the same. But the Hispanic population in this country is young and they're going to have families. Also, I think there are a lot of Hispanic immigrants, so it makes sense that the Hispanic population is going to grow more than any other group.

Speaker 3: You know, these charts are about the whole country, but it really depends on where you live. I live in the city, and the white population is definitely not 70%. I think the African-American population is about 30%. And the Hispanic population is going up, I thinks it's about 20% . . . I'm not sure of those numbers, but there's a good mix. But my parents live in a little town, and it's not very diverse.

Speaker 4: I'm from California, and the population of Asians is much higher there, so I thought the Asian population was 7 or 8%. But now I live in Texas, and my city has a lot of Hispanic people, probably about 40%, and the number is rising. And here we have very few Asians.

Listening 1: Person on the Street (Page 35)

B. Complete. Listen and complete with the vocabulary about population.

1. The Hispanic population is doubling.
2. And the African-American population is remaining about the same.
3. I thought the Asian population was higher.
4. The black population is staying about the same.
5. The Hispanic population is going to grow more than any other group.
6. The Hispanic population is going up.
7. I'm from California, and the population of Asians is much higher there.
8. The number of Hispanics is rising.
9. And here we have very few Asians.

Listening 2: The Census (Page 38)

Every ten years, the United States takes a census of the population. A census counts the number of people who live in each city and state. In 2000, the population of the United States was about 281 million people. By 2050, the population will be over 400 million people. The population is growing by about four million people a year. About three million of this number is from new births, but over one million immigrants enter the United States every year. Eleven percent of the people in the United States were born in another country. More of these immigrants are from Mexico than any other country, at 30% of the immigrant population.

The census gives many interesting facts about the United States. For example, there are more women than men in the United States. For every 100 women, there are only 96 men. The main reason for this is that women live longer than men. What is the life expectancy for men and for women? The life expectancy for women is 80, while the life expectancy for men is 75.

Family life is changing. Americans are waiting longer to get married. The average age for men to marry is 27, while the average age for women is 25. In the past, half of all homes had a mother, a father, and children. Today, only 23% of all homes show this same picture of a married couple with children. Twenty-eight percent of homes have a married couple with no children. Many of these couples are now older and their children have left home. At this time, 12% of all homes are single women, some with young children and some with children who are over 18. Only 4% of homes are single men with children. And almost 25% of Americans live alone.

Americans are on the move. One out of every seven people moves each year. Most people only move a short distance, so they usually stay in the same state. The number one reason that people move is to buy a home, so many of these people are moving from an apartment to a house.

For many years, people in the United States have been moving from the North and the Midwest to the South and the West. States like New York, Pennsylvania, and Massachusetts – all in the North – are growing slowly. States like Florida, Texas, and Nevada – all in the South and the West – are growing very fast. The number one reason is jobs. Many large industries in the North are closing or moving to the South or out of the country. Most new jobs are in the South or West. These areas need workers; they are looking for teachers, builders, cooks, and store workers. The second reason is the weather. More people are retiring and they are choosing warm sunny climates near the coast. Finally, many new immigrants are deciding to live in the South and the West. Many new immigrants already have family and friends in these areas and it is easier to find a job.

C. Note-Taking. Listen to the last part of the talk again. You are going to hear the three reasons that people are moving from the North and the Midwest to the South and the West. Use the words below to help you listen for the reasons.

For many years, people in the United States have been moving from the North and the Midwest to the South and the West. States like New York, Pennsylvania, and Massachusetts – all in the North - are growing slowly. States like Florida, Texas, and Nevada – all in the South and the West - are growing very fast. The number one reason is jobs. Many large industries in the North are closing or moving to the South or out of the country. Most new jobs are in the South or West. These areas need workers; they are looking for teachers, builders, cooks, and store workers. The second reason is the weather. More people are retiring and they are choosing warm sunny climates near the coast. Finally, many new immigrants are deciding to live in the South and the West. Many new immigrants already have family and friends in these areas and it is easier to find a job.

Structure (Page 40)

B. Dictation   Listen and write the sentences you hear.

1. The population is growing by about four million people a year.
2. Over one million immigrants enter the United States every year.
3. There are more women than men in the United States.
4. Americans are waiting longer to get married.
5. Most people only move a short distance.
6. Many of these people are moving from an apartment to a house.

Pronunciation (Page 41)

Pronunciation note: Years and numbers

It takes practice to understand and say years and large numbers.

Years
  nineteen fifty (1950)
  nineteen eighty (1980)
  two thousand (2000)
  two thousand four (2004)
  twenty ten (2010)
Numbers
  four hundred thousand (400,000)
  twenty million, four hundred thousand (20,400,000)
  one hundred twenty million, four hundred thousand (120,400,000)

A. Listen and Complete   The chart shows the population of the United States from 1900 to 2006. Listen and complete the information. You will hear each sentence twice.

In 1900, the population of the United States was 76,100,000.
In 1910, the population of the United States was 92,400,000.
In 1920, the population of the United States was 106,500,000.
In 1930, the population of the United States was 123,100,000.
In 1940, the population of the United States was 132,500,000.
In 1950, the population of the United States was 152,300,000.
In 1960, the population of the United States was 180,700,000.
In 1970, the population of the United States was 205,100,000.
In 1980, the population of the United States was 227,700,000.
In 1990, the population of the United States was 249,900,000.
In 2000, the population of the United States was 281,400,000.
In 2006, the population of the United States reached 300,000,000.

Listening 3: How Do You Like It Here? (Page 42)

Conversation 1

A: When you came to the United States, why did you settle in California?
B: My brother lives here.
A: How do you like it here?
B: Well, I like the weather. But I can't find a job. I'm going to move to Nevada this summer.

Conversation 2

A: Why did you decide to live in Dallas?
B: I have a lot of friends here.
A: How do you like this area?
B: For me, I like it. I have a job and my kids like their school.
A: Are you going to stay here?
B: I sure am.

Conversation 3

A: How do you like Boston?
B: It's too cold.
A: Yeah, it is cold here.
B: When I finish school, I'm going to move to Arizona. I have a cousin there.

Conversation 4

A: How do you like New York?
B: This is the city for me. I really like it here. There are restaurants, museums, and two baseball teams. There's always something to do.
A: Is your family here?
B: Yes, my brother and sister live here, too.

Conversation 5

A: Why did you decide to live in New Jersey?
B: Well, I was living in Pennsylvania, not in a city, but in a little town. But no one spoke Spanish there. I didn't feel comfortable.
A: Who told you about New Jersey?
B: A friend. She said that a lot of Spanish people live here. So, I moved and I really like it here.

Conversation 6

A: I hear you're retiring.
B: Yes, after 25 years at the company.
A: Are you going to stay here in Chicago?
B: It's too expensive here . . . and too cold. We're moving to Florida. We bought a nice house in a retirement community down there.

Unit 5: Starting Your Own Business

Listening 1: Three Small Business Owners (Page 46)

Speaker 1: I have a house cleaning business. It's me and three women. Each day, we clean about five houses. We work together well and we all have specific jobs in each house, like one person does the kitchen, another cleans the bathrooms, another person dusts and vacuums. I have 35 customers and a waiting list of four people who want us, but I don't have time in my schedule.

Speaker 2: My wife and I have a coffee cart business. We work in a big office building that has fifteen floors. When I get off the elevator at each floor, I ring a bell and the workers come and they buy coffee, or tea, or juice and . . . muffins. My wife gets up at 4:00 every morning and makes 300 muffins. People *love* her muffins. Every day she makes blueberry and corn – they're the best selling, and then she makes a special flavor, a different one each day, like raspberry or apple or chocolate chip. And in the afternoon, I do the same thing, but this time, I sell her homemade cookies.

Speaker 3: I have a real estate business. I help people sell their homes and help other people find homes. I love my job. But there's so much paper work and so many phone calls – I work with the buyers, and the sellers, and the lawyers, the bankers, home inspectors. I'm busy all the time. During the week, I take care of paperwork. And on the weekends, I'm usually showing people houses.

Listening 2: Mr. Fix It (Page 48)

Speaker 1: Hey, Jake, I was just speakin' with the boss. He told me you're leaving - at the end of the month?

Jake: Yup - I finally did it. I'm starting my own business.

Speaker 1: Your own business? A construction business? You're gonna build houses, like this one?

Jake: No. No more big jobs. I'm going to be a handyman – I'm going to take small jobs in people's homes. You know, I'll install windows and doors, put in kitchen cabinets, tile bathroom floors.

Speaker 1: What area will you work in?

Jake: I'm going to work right here, in this area. I know lots of people here. I checked it out . . . In this town there is only one handyman, and he has so much business, he can't handle all his calls.

Speaker 1: What about a truck?

Jake: I bought one. A used one. It's at the paint shop now. I'm going to call the business *Mr. Fix It*, so they're painting a sign on both sides of the truck and on the back with the telephone number.

Speaker 1: You've been a carpenter for . . how long? Five years, isn't it. You probably have the tools you need.

Jake: Yeah, I've got everything.

Speaker 1: Don't you have to do all kinds of legal stuff?

Jake: I saw a lawyer a few months ago. He helped me fill out all the paperwork. So now I have a business identification number and a business permit for this area. I need accident insurance, I don't have that yet.

Speaker 1: How about the bank?

Jake: I started a bank account in the name of the business last week. I'm waiting for the checks and a credit card. And Pete, you know Pete Williams, the owner of the hardware store in town? He's going to set up an account for me there. I'll get most of my supplies from him.

Speaker 1: Do you have all the forms you need yet?

Jake: I can order everything on the Internet, like the job estimate forms and the bills. And I'm going to order business cards. I'll give you some when I get them. And next month I'm going to place advertisements in the two local newspapers.

Speaker 1: You should do well. You do great work.

Jake: I hope so. I think I can earn more money if I work for myself. It's going to be a lot of work, but, it's time.

Speaker 1: Good luck!

Pronunciation (Page 51)

Pronunciation Note: *going to - gonna*	
In spoken English, *going to* sounds like *gonna*.	
He's *going to* order business cards.	He's *gonna* order business cards.
I'm *going to* start my own business.	I'm *gonna* start my own business.

A. Listen and Repeat Listen and repeat the sentences.

1. Jake is going to start his own business.
2. He's going to begin next month.
3. He's going to work very hard.
4. I'm going to call Jake.
5. He's going to give me an estimate for a new kitchen window.

Page 51

B. Dictation Listen and write the sentences you hear.

1. I'm going to start my own business.
2. I'm going to earn more money.
3. The bank is going to send me a credit card.
4. I'm going to order the forms I need.
5. My neighbor is going to call Jake.
6. He's going to ask him to tile a floor.

Listening 3: The Customers (Page 52)

Job 1

A: Jake, we'd like an estimate for our bathroom floor. We'd like a tile floor. We already have the tile . . .

B: Let's see . . . The job will take about two days. It should be between $800 and $900. I'll send you an exact estimate.

A: Could you do the work next week?

B: Next week is good.

Job 2

A: Jake, we'd like you to install a door.

B: This should be no problem. It's the right size.

A: How much would it cost?

B: Seventy-five dollars.

A: When can you come?

B: Next Tuesday. Is morning okay?

A: Yes, that's good.

Job 3

A: Here's the problem . . . We had a leak in here last month and now we need some work on the ceiling. Can you fix just that area of the ceiling?

B: Yes. I can fix that area.

A: Great . . How much would that be?

B: It'll be about $200. And do you want it painted, too?

A: No, I'll paint it. When would you be able to start?

B: I could do this about two weeks from now.

A: Okay.

Unit 6: Jobs for the Future

Listening 1: Person on the Street (Page 56)

Interview Questions: What career are you studying for?

What is the job outlook for that career?

Speaker 1: I'm studying nursing. There are always going to be sick people and there are always going to be new babies. And in my nursing program now, the students who are graduating have several job offers. Some of them even got signing bonuses, one girl got a signing bonus of $5,000!

Speaker 2: I'm studying accounting. I think there's a great future for this job. Every company, it doesn't matter if it's large or small, needs an accountant or accounting services.

Speaker 3: Hmmm . . . I want to work in the music business, like selling CDs. Maybe have a music store. A lot of people like music, so I think that would be a real good business to be in.

Listening 2: Jobs for the Future (Page 58)

A. Listen for the Main Idea. Listen to the beginning of the talk. Complete the information.

Each year, the United States government publishes the *Occupational Outlook Handbook*. This large book lists over 250 kinds of jobs. It describes job duties, working conditions, education needed, and salary. It also gives the job outlook, that is, it tells how many openings there will be for each job in the coming years. The job outlook may be average, better than average, or below average. Using the information from the *Occupational Outlook Handbook*, this talk will look at the job outlook for seven jobs. It will explain the reasons why the number of jobs is growing or falling.

Listening 2: Jobs for the Future (Page 58)

Let's begin with bank tellers. The job outlook for bank tellers is below average. Bank tellers help customers; for example, they cash checks or accept deposits. There will be fewer job openings for bank tellers because more people are now using ATM machines and in the future, more customers will do their banking on the Internet.

Next, computer workers. All companies depend on computers, so the number of computer jobs will continue to grow. For example, companies need computer support specialists who help employees with their computer problems and teach them to use the company's software. Most computer workers have an excellent job future.

How about the men and women who deliver our mail? They are mail carriers. These workers have a poor job future. Companies are using e-mail and fax machines to send information and people are buying stamps at stores. On the other hand, the job outlook for delivery workers is above average. People are buying more items on the Internet and these companies deliver small packages directly to a customer's home.

The fastest growing group of workers is health care workers. The job outlook for these workers, such as nurses, x-ray technicians, and physical therapists, is excellent. The population is increasing and people are living longer. In the future, more than one half of all new jobs will be in the health care industry.

What is the job outlook for travel agents? Millions of people travel for business and for pleasure. The number of retired people is growing and many of them will take two vacations a year. However, more and more people are using the Internet to make airline reservations, rent cars, and make their own travel plans, so the job outlook for travel agents is below average.

Finally, the job outlook for teachers is good. The school population is increasing and many teachers who are in their forties and fifties will retire in the next ten years. Schools are having a difficult time finding teachers in math, science and foreign language, so teachers in those subject areas will be in demand.

The *Occupational Outlook Handbook* is in the reference section of the library and it is available on the Internet. It can tell you if the work you are interested in has a good future or not.

Structure (Page 60)

A. Dictation   Listen and write the sentences you hear.

1. More people are using ATM machines.
2. There will be fewer openings for bank tellers.
3. People are buying their stamps at stores.

4. People will take more vacations.
5. Many teachers will retire in the next ten years.
6. The number of computer jobs will continue to grow.

Pronunciation (Page 61–62)

> Pronunciation note: Salaries
> It will take time and practice to be able to say salaries in English.
> $28,000/year (twenty-eight thousand a year)
> $450/week (four hundred fifty dollars a week)
> $20/hour (twenty dollars an hour)
> $9.50/hour (nine-fifty an hour)

A. Listen for Numbers   This is a list of the average salary for eight jobs. Listen and complete the information. You will hear each sentence twice.

1. The average salary for a bank teller is between $18,000 and $24,000.
2. A computer support specialist earns between $32,000 and $53,000.
3. The average salary for a mail carrier is about $41,000.
4. A delivery worker makes about $12.00 an hour.
5. The average salary for a licensed practical nurse is $34,000.
6. A registered nurse earns about $52,000.
7. A travel agent makes between $21,000 and $35,000.
8. The average salary for a teacher is about $47,000.

Listening 3: How's Business? (Page 63)

Conversation 1

A: Business is really slow.
B: Yeah?
A: My company laid off three more people last week.
B: In your department?
A: Yeah. I hope I'm not the next.

Conversation 2

A: How's your new job?
B: I like it.
A: What do you do?
B: I just stand at the door and check ID cards.

Conversation 3

A: I have lots of free time now. I'm on unemployment.
B: What happened?
A: My company moved to Korea. Everybody got laid off.

Conversation 4

A: I'm taking a computer course.
B: How come? Did you lose your job?
A: No, but my boss is 68 . . . 69 years old. I think he'll retire in a year or two. Then, I don't know what's going to happen.
B: So, you want to be ready.

A: Yeah.

Conversation 5

A: I fill out one or two job applications a week, but no one's hiring.

B: I hear they're looking for school bus drivers at the Yellow Bus Company.

A: Oh, yeah? Do you know what they're paying?

B: My cousin works there. I think they pay about fourteen dollars an hour.

A: Thanks. I'll look into it.

Conversation 6

A: My company hired 15 new workers last year.

B: What kind of company is that?

A: It's a home health care company. We work with the elderly and with people who just came out of the hospital, you know, like after an operation or a heart attack.

B: Why did you need so many people?

A: Well, there are a lot more older people. And we have a good reputation. People know we give really good care.

Unit 7: A Professional

Listening 1: Person on the Street (Page 68)

Interview Question: Were you ever robbed?

Speaker 1: We were away from home for a week and came back and walked into the house and everything, our bedroom, was turned upside down, our dining room, things were all over the floor. . . . The robber took jewelry and money. And you won't believe this, but we had cookies in the kitchen and the robber opened the box and ate some of the cookies. He got in through the side door. He left through the back door and then went to our neighbors and robbed our neighbors, too.

Speaker 2: Yes. One time I was walking home with my boyfriend and this guy, he came up in his car and, he got out of the car and he had a gun. We were on a quiet street and no one else was around. We gave him whatever money we had and then he stole my boyfriend's leather jacket. It was so fast. It was like eight, nine o'clock at night in the fall.

Speaker 3: Yeah, I was robbed. I was, uh, about twenty-two, still living at home. I was living with my mother and I was home alone. And I heard someone in the house. And I ran out of the house and to the neighbors and I called the police. The cops came . . . and the guy who broke into the house, I guess he heard me and he ran away and didn't take anything.

Listening 2: A Professional (Page 70)

Richard Williams works hard. He's intelligent, careful, and fast. His work is dangerous. Richard thinks of himself as a professional, a professional thief.

Yesterday was a typical day. Richard dressed in a business suit, took his briefcase, and drove to a town about ten miles from his home. He parked his car in a busy area, then began to walk along the street. He was just another businessman, walking to work.

At 8:00, Richard saw what he wanted. A man was leaving his house. Richard walked around the block again. At 8:05, he watched a woman leave the same house. After she left, Richard worked quickly. He walked to the side of the house and stood behind a tree. He took a screwdriver out of his briefcase and quickly opened the window and climbed in. First, he looked through the desk in the living room. He found $500 in cash. In the dining room, he put the silverware into his briefcase. The next stop was the bedroom. Richard stole a diamond ring and a gold necklace. He also took a camera. Richard passed a TV, a stereo, and a computer, but he didn't touch them. Everything had to fit into his briefcase. In less than five minutes, Richard climbed back out the window. He looked around carefully, then began his walk down the street again. No one looked at him. He was just another businessman, walking to work.

Structure (Page 72)

A. Dictation Listen and write the sentences you hear.

1. Richard walked along the street.
2. He looked like a professional.
3. He carried a briefcase.
4. Richard climbed in the window.
5. He looked through the desk in the living room.
6. He only stayed in the house for five minutes.

Pronunciation (Page 73)

A. -ed Endings Say each of these past tense verbs to yourself. Before you listen, decide if the verb has one or two syllables. Then, listen to the pronunciation of each verb and write the number of syllables you hear.

1. parked
2. wanted
3. dressed
4. worked
5. needed
6. passed
7. climbed
8. waited
9. walked
10. started
11. robbed
12. carried

Pronunciation Note: Linking with -ed
When a final -ed is followed by a word that begins with a vowel, the sounds are linked. The -d sounds like part of the next word.
He watched a [these as one word] woman leave the house.

B. Linking with -ed Listen carefully and complete these sentences with the missing words. Mark the linking sounds.

1. He parked on Main Street.
2. He dressed in a business suit.
3. He walked around the block.
4. He passed a color TV.

5. He worked in the morning.
6. He carried a briefcase.
7. He opened a window.
8. He climbed in.
9. He robbed a house every day.

Listening 3: The End of Richard's Career (Page 74)

Conversation 1

OFFICER: Mr. Jackson, we just checked around the outside of your house.

MR. JACKSON: How did the thief get in?

OFFICER: The thief got in through the side window.

MR. JACKSON: The side window?

OFFICER: Yes, we found footprints under the window and there's dirt on the carpet, in the living room. And there are marks on the window outside. He probably used a screwdriver to open the window. Now, what did he take?

MR. JACKSON: Our cash. We had about $500 in the desk.

MRS. JACKSON: And he took my jewelry. My diamond ring and gold necklace are gone. And he stole the silverware.

MR. JACKSON: He took a camera, too . . . my new digital camera.

MRS. JACKSON: Why didn't he take the computer or the television set?

OFFICER: He was on foot. He only took what he could carry.

Conversation 2

OFFICER: What time did you leave your home this morning?

DANIELLE: Well, I left for work at about 8:30, but when I got to the light, I saw I forgot my briefcase, so I drove back home. And when I drove in the driveway, I saw a man run out the front door.

OFFICER: Which way did he go?

DANIELLE: He ran up the street and he jumped into a car, it was a black car, and he drove away fast.

OFFICER: Did you get the license plate number?

DANIELLE: No, he was too far away. But the car was new. It was a . . . it was a big car, I think it was a Cadillac.

OFFICER: Did you get a good look at him?

DANIELLE: No, not really. He was tall and thin. He was white and he had brown hair. And he was wearing a business suit.

OFFICER: Did he take anything?

DANIELLE: I don't think he had time to take anything. I think I surprised him.

Conversation 3

OFFICER: Do you live here?

ARTHUR: No, I'm visiting my brother. My brother and his wife left for work at 7:30. A few minutes later, somebody got into the house. I guess he thought the house was empty.

OFFICER: Where were you?

ARTHUR: I was in the kitchen. I heard something in the living room, so I got up to check. And there was this man in the living room, putting money into his briefcase. I guess I surprised him. He ran out the front door and I ran after him.

OFFICER: Did you catch him?

ARTHUR: No, he fell down the steps and broke his leg. That's when I called you.

OFFICER: We've been looking for this man. In the past two weeks, he broke into 20 homes in this area.

Unit 8: The Lottery

Listening 1: Person on the Street (Page 78)

Interview question: What would you do if you won a million dollars?

Speaker 1: Um, I would put most of it away for the future and I would love a new kitchen in our house. And I'd buy some new furniture.

Speaker 2: Um, I'd a I'd a pay off my mortgage. And I'd take my wife and kids on vacation somewhere fun for a week. And the rest of it, we'd put into savings.

Speaker 3: I would buy a home. I'd start a college fund for my son. I'd buy my mother a house. And be sure that my brothers and sisters are taken care of. And then just continue school.

Listening 2: Lottery Winners (Page 80)

Every week, millions of people buy lottery tickets, and every week, there are a few big winners. Let's look at four past winners.

Lisa K. worked as a cashier in a supermarket. She wanted to be an artist, but she didn't have enough money to go to school. In August, Lisa bought one ticket and won two million dollars. She quit her job and is now attending art school. Lisa says, "If I don't become an artist, it's my own fault. I have the opportunity now."

Mark L. was a car salesperson. He worked seven days a week and had little time for family life. Every week, he bought three lottery tickets. One day, he picked the winning numbers and won three million dollars. He quit his job the next day. Now he spends his time bowling, working in the garden, and fixing things in his house. But, he's bored. He doesn't want to sell cars again, but he isn't sure what he wants to do with his life.

Every week for ten years, Mabel S. stopped at the corner store and bought five lottery tickets. She was over 60 years old and retired when she won a million dollars. She started to spend money immediately. She bought a new car, new clothes, and new furniture for her house. She paid her son's college tuition. Then she gave all her grandchildren money. After a few months, she had no money left to pay her bills. Also, she forgot about taxes and didn't have enough money to pay them. She plans to spend her money more carefully next year.

Jack B. only bought a lottery ticket a few times a year. One day when he stopped for gas, he bought a ticket. His winning ticket was worth two million dollars. He is one of the small number of winners who did not quit his job. Jack still teaches English at a high school in his area. But he and his wife now have a new car in the garage. They take their four children on an interesting vacation every year. And they don't worry about sending their children to college. They say that money brings security and gives a person opportunities, but it doesn't bring happiness.

Structure (Page 82)

B. Dictation   Listen and write the sentences you hear. You will hear *doesn't* or *didn't* in each sentence.

1. Mark didn't like his job.
2. He didn't have time to enjoy life.
3. Mark doesn't work anymore.
4. He doesn't want to stay home all the time.
5. He doesn't know what to do with his time.
6. Money doesn't bring happiness.

Pronunciation (Page 82)

Pronunciation Note: Linking with *A/An*

When a final consonant is followed by *a* or *an*, the sounds are linked. The *a* or *an* sounds like part of the word before.

He won a million dollars.

A. Linking with A/An.   Complete these sentences with the missing words. Mark the linking sounds.

1. Lisa was a cashier in a supermarket.
2. She wants to become an artist.
3. Mark was a car salesman.
4. He worked seven days a week.
5. Mabel stopped at a store.
6. She bought a new car.
7. Jack bought a ticket.
8. He teaches at a high school.

9. They have a new car.
10. They take their children on an interesting vacation every year.

Pronunciation (Page 83)

Pronunciation note: Negative contractions
When listening, we often do not hear a full *t* at the end of a negative contraction.
They don't worry about money.
She didn't pay her taxes.

C. Negative Contractions.   Listen and write the negative contraction you hear.

1. She didn't have enough money to go to school.
2. If I don't become an artist, it's my own fault.
3. He didn't have time for family life.
4. He doesn't want to sell cars again.
5. He isn't sure what to do.
6. She didn't have any more money.
7. He didn't quit his job.
8. They don't worry about money.
9. Money doesn't bring happiness.

Listening 3: Do You Ever Buy Lottery Tickets? (Page 84)

Conversation 1

A: Do you ever buy lottery tickets?
B: Yeah, every week. This week, it's up to four million dollars.
A: How much do you spend on tickets?
B: Spend? You mean waste. I buy five tickets a week, five dollars. And I never win a penny. But I still keep buying tickets.

Conversation 2

A: Do you ever buy lottery tickets?
B: Yup. I get paid on Friday. And on the way home, I buy two or three.
A: What numbers do you play?
B: Well, on one ticket, I always play the same number. I put my birthday, my wife's birthday and the kids' birthdays. For the other tickets, I just let the machine pick the numbers.

Conversation 3

A: Do you ever buy lottery tickets?
B: Me, no. But my cousin won the lottery about two years ago.
A: Really?
B: Really. He bought a house with the money. A beautiful big house with four bedrooms and a great kitchen.
A: Did he quit work?
B: No. The money pays the mortgage and taxes and things for the house, but they still have to eat.

Conversation 4

A: Do you ever buy lottery tickets?

B: Well, sometimes. Like if the jackpot is really big, say over ten million, then I buy one or two.

Conversation 5

A: Do you ever buy lottery tickets?

B: I used to. Every week, I bought three. And I did that for about six or seven years. And I never won a penny. And so one day I stopped. I never bought another ticket.

Conversation 6

A: Do you ever buy lottery tickets?

B: Sure, I spend about $10 dollars a week on tickets. I buy a few different kinds of tickets.

A: Did you ever win any money?

B: Yes, a couple of times. Once I won $630 and another time I won almost $2,000.

Conversation 7

A: Do you ever buy lottery tickets?

B: Yup. One ticket every week. I know it's not a lot, but someone's going to win that money and someday, it's going to be me.

Unit 9: Cell Phones

Listening 1: Person on the Street (Page 89)

Interview questions: How long do you talk on your cell phone everyday? Who do you talk to?

Speaker 1: Well, I don't stay on the phone long. But I do call everyone in my family, well maybe seven or eight of them, and have a quick two to three minute chat. I use it when I'm bored and I'm not doing anything, like when I'm riding on the bus. I talk to my cousin, I talk to my mother, I talk to my aunt Vera, and my sister Shirley. I talk to, you know, people like that.

Speaker 2: I have a cell phone, but I hardly ever use it. It's more, like, for emergencies.

Speaker 3: My husband just got mad at me because I went over the limit last month. Let's see, I think it was 80 minutes over the limit. We have 1000 minutes. I usually talk to my mother for, maybe, 30 minutes at a time, and my friends. Anyway, I told him we should get a plan for more minutes.

Speaker 4: I'm always on my cell phone. I talk to my boyfriend, my sisters, my friends. I'm on the phone maybe two, three hours a day. I have two thousand minutes on my cell phone plan, but at night and on the weekends, the minutes are free.

Listening 2: Cell Phones, a Conversation (Page 91)

Speaker 1: Okay. At 5:00? I'll pick you up . . . Right . . . In front of the school. Bye, hon.

Speaker 2: Your son?

Speaker 1: Yeah. He has baseball practice after school today.

Speaker 3: Cell phones . . . we're always connected.

Speaker 4: Uh, huh . . they're good, but they're a pain. Let me tell you, I was at the movies last night. And a girl's cell phone rang. She answered her phone and started talking to a friend . . . in the movie theater!

Speaker 3: What's wrong with people?

Speaker 4: Well, people around her were really annoyed. People turned and looked at her. And someone called out, "Get off the phone!"

Speaker 2: Some people think they can talk anywhere.

Speaker 3: I was on the train last month and the train car was full. This one guy, well, he just bought a car. And I think, he called everyone he knew and told them the same story, the same information about his car. Pretty soon, everyone knew the color, the price, the model. . .

Speaker 1: Did anyone say anything?

Speaker 3: Yeah, but he didn't care.

Speaker 4: You should sit in the *Quiet* car. No one can talk on a cell phone.

Speaker 2: Well, how about restaurants? Last Friday a friend and I went out for dinner at a nice restaurant . . and we were eating dinner . . and the woman at the next table got a phone call. She began to talk with a friend. All about her boyfriend. And she was talking loud.

Speaker 1: Why is it a person on a cell phone never talks quietly?

Speaker 3: I know. They talk so loud . . .

Speaker 2: Well, the waiter came over and asked her to talk outside.

Speaker 4: Bravo!

Speaker 3: I can understand if it's an emergency, like the babysitter or someone like that. Or maybe a doctor is getting an emergency call. But to sit and talk at a table in a restaurant . . .

Speaker 4: Some restaurants are banning cell phones.

Speaker 2: Lots of places should ban them.

Speaker 1: Oh! That reminds me. There's now a sign in my bank, *No Cell Phones*.

Speaker 4: In your bank?

Speaker 1: I asked the teller about it and she said they don't want people to take pictures of other people's checks or account information.

Speaker 3: I guess that's possible. You could even take a short video of someone putting in an ATM number.

Speaker 2: Okay. Whose phone is that?

Pronunciation (Page 94)

> Pronunciation note: Word stress
>
> In a conversation, people stress words that are important or that give their story special emphasis. Stressed words are said longer and more loudly.

A. Word Stress. Listen and underline the stressed word or words in each sentence.

1. She answered the phone and started talking to a friend <u>in the movie theater</u>.
2. What's <u>wrong</u> with people?
3. He called everyone he knew and told them the <u>same</u> story, the <u>same</u> information about his car.
4. Well, how about <u>restaurants</u>?
5. A person on a cell phone <u>never</u> talks quietly.
6. I know. They talk so <u>loud</u>.
7. Well, the waiter came over and asked her to talk <u>out-side</u>.
8. I can understand if it's an <u>emergency</u>.
9. There's now a sign in my <u>bank</u>, *No Cell Phones*.

Listening 3: Telephone Conversations (Page 95)

Conversation 1

w: Hi, hon. Busy?
m: Hi. Yeah. Lots of customers today.
w: Did that big order of cameras finally arrive?
m: Yeah. We're unpacking it in the back. Kids home yet?
w: They're in the living room. They're doing their homework.
m: Good. I'll be home around 6:00.
w: We're having chicken and rice for dinner. Could you stop on the way home and pick up a vegetable for dinner? Anything you like – broccoli, green beans, peas, whatever.
m: Sure.

Conversation 2

M1: Hey, George. Bill here.
M2: Hey, Bill. What's up?
M1: A couple of the guys, Pete, Luis, Junior, we're getting together tomorrow afternoon. We're going watch the big game on TV.
M2: Where? At your house?
M1: Mmh-mmh. Over here. I have the biggest TV.
M2: What can I bring?

M1: Just some soda. We'll all chip in and order some pizza.
M2: Sounds good. What time?
M1: The game starts at 2:00. Anytime between 1:30 and 2:00 would be good.

Conversation 3

w: Hello.
m: Mrs. Bigsley, this is Tim Summers, from Apex Life Insurance.
w: Yes. Hi, Tim.
m: We have an appointment this afternoon.
w: Yes, at 2:00.
m: I'm running a little late because the traffic is terrible. I think there's an accident. Would 3:00 be okay with you?
w: 3:00? No, I have a short meeting at 3:00. How about 4:00?
m: 4:00 is good. I'll see you then.
w: Okay. 4:00.

Conversation 4:

1: Hey, Emma.
2: Hi, Jen.
1: I'm at Shopper's World. I'm trying on this dress . . but I'm not sure . . .
2: Send me a picture.
1: I took it already. I'm sending it to you now.
2: Got it. I like the dress. It's great. But I don't know about the color. It's kind of dark. Is it really that dark? Like a brown?
1: Yeah, I'm not sure about the color either.
2: Do they have it in a lighter color? Like maybe beige?
1: I'm going to keep looking. . . call you back.

Unit 10: Carjackings

Listening 1: Person on the Street (Page 100)

Interview Question: When you get in your car, do you lock your doors right away?

Speaker 1: Hmm. Yeah, I'd have to say that I lock them Not right away, but after I pull out of my driveway or my parking space, I lock them.

Speaker 2: No, no, I don't even think about locking doors.

Speaker 3: I don't have to think about it. As soon as I start to drive, the doors lock automatically.

Speaker 4: No, I probably should. No, unless . . . I really don't do that unless I'm driving through some part of town I'm really not comfortable with. Generally, no.

Listening 2: Two Carjackings (Page 102)

Story 1

Speaker 1: "Did you hear what happened at Abby's grocery last night?

Speaker 2: No . . What happened?

Speaker 1: Some guys stole a car.

Speaker 2: No way . . .

Speaker 1: Well, see, this guy, he goes into the grocery store, like . .uh, just to buy some bread or somethin' . . and he walks out to the parking lot, he gets in his car . . . Then, he starts his car, puts it in reverse and starts to back up. But then he sees, like, this paper or something on the back window. So, he gets out of his car, and walks around to the back of the car to, you know, to take the paper off the window, and then, like, these two guys, they jump into his car, and they drive away. They almost hit him.

Speaker 2: You're kidding!

Speaker 1: My sister was there when the guy comes running back into the store, yelling "Some guys just stole my car!"

Speaker 2: Whoa!

Speaker 1: Yeah. The owner called the police.

Speaker 2: Did your sister see the guys?

Speaker 1: Nah. She didn't see anyone. Just the man.

Speaker 2: Someone from around here?

Speaker 1: She, like, didn't know him or anything.

Speaker 2: Whoa!

Story 2

Speaker 1: You know the gas station on Broad Street, the one near the library?

Speaker 2: Yes.

Speaker 1: Let me tell you what happened yesterday, in broad daylight, in the middle of the afternoon!

Speaker 2: Oh, dear. What happened?

Speaker 1: Well, one of the women from town stopped at the gas station to get some gas. And she opened her wallet and she only had a ten-dollar bill, so she only got ten dollars worth of gas. Then, she went inside and paid the cashier and went back outside and got in her car. And, thank goodness, she locked her car door . . because, as she was pulling away, a man, a well-dressed man, friendly looking, walked up to her window and said, "Excuse me, ma'am. You dropped this when you were in the store." And he showed her a five-dollar bill. Well, she knew she didn't have a five, she only had that ten, so she shook her head and said, "Sorry, that's not mine." Well, the man began to hit the car window and he tried to open her door. Can you believe it? Well, the woman drove away fast and she went right to the police station. And they told her she was lucky . . . that in the past month, this carjacker had stolen four cars this way. Now, why haven't we been told about this in the newspapers!? This could happen to any of us!

Page 103

C. Extra Words These sentences have several "extra" words. Listen and give the idea of each sentence. (Do not complete the sentences.)

1. Well, see, this guy, he goes into the grocery, like . .uh, just to buy some bread or something.
2. And then he sees, like, this paper or something on the back window.
3. So, he gets out of his car, and walks around to the back of the car to, you know, to take the paper off the window.
4. And then, like, these two guys, they jump into his car, and they drive away.

Structure (Page 104)

A. Dictation Listen and write the sentences you hear.

1. A man got into his car.
2. He saw a piece of paper on his back window.
3. He walked around to the back of the car.
4. Two men jumped into his car.
5. They drove away with his car.
6. The man called the police.

Pronunciation (Page 105)

> **Pronunciation Note: h in his, him, and her**
>
> We hear the h in his, him, and her when it is the first word in a sentence.
>
> We often do not hear the h in his, him, and her when it follows another word.
>
> He gets in his car.
>
> She didn't know him.   She locked her car door

A. His/Him/Her. Listen and repeat the sentences. Listen for the linking in each sentence.

1. He gets in his car.
2. He gets out of his car.
3. These two guys jump in his car.
4. They almost hit him.
5. She didn't know him.
6. She got in her car.
7. She locked her car door.
8. He showed her a five-dollar bill.
9. He tried to open her door.
10. They told her she was lucky.

Listening 3: A Description (Page 106)

Speaker 1: I can't believe this. The man looked nice. Well dressed, a short sleeve shirt and a tie.

Speaker 2: Can you describe him?

Speaker 1: Yes. I saw him very well. He was white, young, maybe about 30 to 35 years old. He was tall and kind of thin. He was about my husband's height, that's six feet tall, but not as heavy . . . .probably about 170 pounds. He had short brown hair . . very short . . . light brown.

Speaker 2: Think about his face. Did he have a moustache . . a beard?

Speaker 1: No moustache or beard. But now I think of it, I remember his ears. I know this is funny, but he had big ears. And he had an earring in one ear.

Speaker 2: Gold? Silver?

Speaker 1: A little stone, maybe a diamond.

Speaker 2: How about glasses? Was he wearing sunglasses?

Speaker 1: Umm . . yes, sunglasses. But light sunglasses, not those real dark ones.

Speaker 2: Do you remember anything about his clothes?

Speaker 1: Well, he was wearing a short sleeve shirt . . blue. A dress shirt, not a t-shirt. And a tie, but I don't remember the color. Beige pants. He looked like a businessman, you know, going to see his next client or to a meeting.

Speaker 2: Did you look back at him when you were driving away?

Speaker 1: I looked back once in my rearview mirror . . I was scared that he was going to follow me. He was running toward the highway.

Speaker 2: We're trying to get a good idea of what this man looked like. We'd like to put up a poster in the post office and the stores in this area. We have a police artist in the county. If we had the artist come in, do you think you could work with him . . . describe the man . . .see if we could get a good picture of him.

Speaker 1: Yes, I think I could do that.

Unit 11 You're Fired!

Listening 1: Person on the Street (Page 110)

Interview Question: Did anyone at your job ever get fired?

Person 1

A: Where do you work?
B: At Gino's Supermarket.
A: Did anyone at your job ever get fired?
B: Yes. "No call, no show . . . no job. If you can't come to work, you just have to call and say, "I'm not coming in." And some people don't even do that. Like Monday, this new cashier didn't show up, and when she came in on Tuesday, they fired her.

Person 2

A: Where do you work?
B: For Yellow Cab. I'm a taxi driver.
A: Did anyone at your job ever get fired?
B: We had this one driver who was always getting tickets, tickets for parking and tickets for speeding. But the boss didn't fire him because he was his cousin. But then, he was in an accident. It wasn't a bad accident, but it was his fault. The boss fired him the same day.

Person 3

A: Where do you work?
B: At a clothing store . . . a men's clothing store.
A: Did anyone at your job ever get fired?
B: Sure. Last month the boss fired this guy. He was fired for stealing [stealin']. It was a clothing store. He tried to steal clothes and he got caught. He was leaving the store and that little beeping [beepin'] thing went off, you know, like it's a little alarm and he got caught. The boss said, "You're fired. Just leave."

Listening 2: The Dentist and the Dental Hygienist (Page 112)

First, listen to Dr. Park.

I'm a dentist. In my office, there are five office workers and two dental hygienists. Today I fired Shelly, one of the hygienists. Shelly is a wonderful young woman, friendly, talkative, and a very good hygienist. But, she was bringing her personal life into the office. She was always coming in late or leaving early. And she was calling in sick two or three times a month. I never knew if she was coming in to work or not. Shelly was having problems with her boyfriend and her mother was sick. So, while she was cleaning people's teeth or taking x-rays, she was telling her patients all about her personal life. Last week, I walked into the examining room and Shelly was crying and her patient was, too. Well, I'm sorry, but I think people need to have a home life and a work life. Don't bring your problems at home into the office. I spoke with Shelly at her evaluation two months ago and told her that she was out of the office too much. I said, Shelly, we can change your schedule. If you want, take one day off a week and work on Saturdays. But, she didn't want to. She wanted to spend the weekends with her boyfriend. Also, last week the other dental hygienist complained to me about Shelly. When Shelly leaves early, she has to work overtime and take Shelly's patients. I need a dental hygienist I can depend on. I called Shelly into my office today and fired her.

Now, listen to Shelly.

I can't believe this. I got fired today. I'm a dental hygienist and I'm very good at my job. I do a very good cleaning and my patients are happy with my work. I've worked at Doctor Park's office for three years, and this whole time, he only received one or two complaints about me. Okay, I know I am having problems at home. I think my boyfriend is seeing another woman and my mother has a lot of medical problems, so a few times a month, I left early to take her to the doctor, but the other hygienist took my patients. She never complained to *me* about it. And the patients, I love my patients. I don't think of them as patients, I think of them as friends. When they asked me, *How are you*, I knew they wanted to hear about my boyfriend and my mother. The doctor said that I was always calling in sick. I only called in sick two or three times a month. What am I going to do? I really need this job.

Structure (Page 114)

A. Dictation   Listen and write the sentences you hear.

1. Shelly was calling in sick two or three times a month.
2. I think people need a home life and a personal life
3. Don't bring your problems at home into the office.
4. If you want, we can change your schedule.
5. I need a person I can depend on.
6. I called Shelly into my office today and fired her.

Pronunciation (Page 115)

Pronunciation Note: Linking

Linking means joining or saying together. Link the final consonant of a word with the beginning vowel in the next word.

Comes in late

Three times a month

Work on Saturday

A. Linking   Listen and repeat these short phrases and sentences.

1. come in late
2. call in sick
3. three times a month
4. work overtime
5. depend on
6. problems at home
7. I'm a dentist.
8. She's a good hygienist.
9. Take one day off a week.
10. My patients are happy.

Listening 3: Calling in Sick (Page 116)
Call 1
A: Barker Industries. Mr. Barker speaking.

B: Hello, Mr. Barker. This is Jim. I can't come to work today. I have a high fever. I'm going to the doctor later.

A: Okay, Jim. Feel better.

B: Thanks, Mr. Barker.

Call 2
A: Nola Electronics. This is Cindy Waters.

B: Hi Cindy. It's Ann.

A: Hi Ann. What's happening?

B: Cindy, I missed the train.

A: Where are you now?

B: I'm home.

A: Are you coming in today?

B: No, I'm staying home.

A: Okay. I'll tell Mr. Cooper.

Call 3
A: Garcia Painting. This is Sam Garcia speaking.

B: Hi . . Mr. Garcia. This is Matt. Matt Brown.

A: Hi, Matt.

B: I have a problem. My son was walking to school this morning, and he fell and broke his arm. I'm at the hospital with him now, in the emergency room.

A: Okay. I'll ask another employee to work overtime. Just take care of your son.

Call 4
A: A-1 Computer. Leah Mason speaking. How can I help you?

B: Hello. This is Celia. Celia Hong.

A: Hello, Celia.

B: Leah, could you speak with Mrs. Davis? When I was driving to work today, I got a flat tire. . . . My car went out of control, and I hit another car. Everybody is okay, but everything is a mess with the cars and the police.

A: Celia, Mrs. Davis isn't in yet. I'll leave her the message.

B: Thank you.

Unit 12: The Titanic

Listening 1: Person on the Street (Page 121)

Interview Question: How many continents are there?

Speaker 1: How many continents? Five. I'm sure that there are five continents. The Americas, Africa, Oceania, Antarctica, and Europe and Asia. No,no, that's six and I'm sure there are five. I'm lost. No, I have it. Europe and Asia are one. Yes, that's right. It's one continent, Eurasia. So, yes, there are five.

Speaker 2: We learned there are five continents. America . . ..Africa .. Asia .. Europe . . and Oceania. No, Antarctica is not a continent because nobody lives there. America is one continent. It's divided into North America, and Central America, and South America, but you count it as one continent. And Europe and Asia? They are two separate continents.

Speaker 3: There are seven continents. North America, South America. No, they're not the same, they're two different continents. And then there is Europe, Asia, Africa, and Australia and Antarctica. That's it. Seven.

Listening 2: The Titanic Disaster (Page 123)

Millionaire Arthur Ryerson stepped on board the Titanic, the world's most famous luxury ship. He was going to enjoy this trip across the Atlantic. This was the first voyage for the Titanic, a trip from England to New York City. Her decks were filled with libraries, smoking rooms, dining rooms, a gymnasium, and a swimming pool.

When the Titanic left England on April 10, 1912, she was carrying 2,224 passengers and crew. The first four days of the trip were clear, calm, and cold. Arthur Ryerson spent his days talking, walking, and playing cards with several of his friends. All the passengers were enjoying their days aboard the ship. None of them knew of the danger ahead. They were approaching icebergs.

The evening of April 14 was relaxed and friendly. By 11:30, most passengers were sleeping or getting ready for bed. Other passengers were reading, drinking, or writing letters. The band was finishing for the evening. Arthur Ryerson was playing cards with three of his friends.

Out in the cold, one of the crewmen was standing watch. Suddenly, up ahead, he saw something in the water. He immediately rang three bells and called the engine room. "Iceberg, right ahead! Stop!" It was too late. The iceberg ripped a 300-foot hole in the right side of the Titanic. The ship was filling with water and sinking fast.

Arthur Ryerson was one of the men who helped women and children into the lifeboats. When he saw there would be no room for himself or any of the other men on the ship, Ryerson and his three friends returned to the smoking room and their game of cards. They were still playing as the Titanic sank into the icy waters. On that cold evening in 1912, 1,513 people lost their lives in one of the worst sea disasters in history.

D. Listen for Meaning. Listen to these sentences from the beginning of the story. You may understand some of the words, but not all of them. Circle the correct meaning of the sentence.

1. Millionaire Arthur Ryerson stepped on board the Titanic, the world's most famous luxury ship. He was going to enjoy this trip across the Atlantic.
2. This was the first voyage for the Titanic, a trip from England to New York.

3. Her decks were filled with libraries, smoking rooms, dining rooms, a gymnasium, and a swimming pool.
4. When the Titanic left England on April 10, 1912, she was carrying 2,224 passengers and crew.
5. The first four days of the trip were clear, calm, and cold.
6. None of the passengers knew of the danger ahead. They were approaching icebergs.

Structure (Page 125)

A. Dictation   Listen and write the sentences you hear. In all the sentences, the verb is in the past continuous tense.

1. The ship was carrying 2,224 passengers.
2. The passengers were enjoying the trip.
3. The ship was approaching icebergs.
4. Many passengers were getting ready for bed.
5. One of the crewmen was standing watch.
6. The ship was sinking fast.

Pronunciation (Page 126)

Listening note: *of*

We often do not hear the *f* in the word *of.*

the decks of the ship — the decks of the ship

Before a vowel or an *h, f* sounds like *v.*

of April — ov April

three of his friends - three ov his friends

A. Of.   Listen carefully and complete these sentences.

1. The Titanic pulled out of port on April 10, 1912.
2. The first four days of the trip were clear and cold.
3. Arthur Ryerson was playing cards with several of his friends.
4. None of them knew of the danger ahead.
5. The evening of April 14 was relaxed.
6. He was in a smoking room with three of his friends.
7. One of the crewmen was standing watch.
8. There was no room for any of the men.
9. He returned to his game of cards.
10. It was one of the worst sea disasters in history.

Listening 3: A Cruise to Alaska (Page 127)

We went to Alaska. It was the most interesting cruise I've ever been on, not the most relaxing, but the most interesting. The scenery was fabulous, so different than anything I've ever seen.

We took a plane to Vancouver and we picked up the ship there.

It was a nine day cruise. You stay on the ship the whole time. You pull into different ports and you have shore excursions.

Not too big. Probably about 1,200 passengers.

The excursions were wonderful. One day, we got onto a smaller boat and went whale watching. We saw fifteen, twenty whales. They came very near our boat. And they were jumping out of the water. And one day my husband went salmon fishing and caught three or four salmon. And we went to a glacier walk, and walked on the glacier. We had such an interesting time.

Well, the weather wasn't great. It was never warm, usually cool. And it rained a lot.

Well, you know, they always have different activities. I took a couple of yoga classes. And every day, there were different lectures about Alaska, like, the animals, the history. And they had these shows at night, they were spectacular. And there's music, dancing. They also show movies. The ship had its own little movie theater.

I don't remember how many lifeboats, but there were definitely enough. At the beginning of the cruise, they had this, what do you call it, this practice exercise when you put on your lifejacket. And, uh, you go to your exit area. And they explained that they had lifeboats for everyone. We knew exactly which area to go to, how to put on the life vest, and they show you, I don't know, what you're supposed to do. They do that every cruise.

You need to be careful with the price of a cruise. At first, it sounded reasonable, I think it was about $1000 a person. Remember, the rooms are all different prices, depending on the size and location. And the price also depends on the date; you can sometimes get very good deals. But, the excursions can double the price. They are so expensive. Some excursions are only fifty or sixty dollars, but a lot of them are over $100 and some are $200 or more each person. So soon, your trip begins to get very expensive. It was more than we expected.

Unit 13: Dreams

Listening 1: Person on the Street (Page 133)

Interview Questions:

Do you dream?

Did you dream last night?

Do you think that dreams have any meaning?

Speaker 1: I *did* dream and I remember thinking about it in the morning, like, when I woke up, but now that the day is passed, I don't really remember, . . not really. I . . . I . . . When I first wake up, I think about them . . my dreams. But as the day goes on, I forget about them. I think some dreams, are like, things that you want to do in life or something that's important to you. And some dreams, are like, what is *this*?

Speaker 2: Did I dream last night? I might have, but I don't remember. I think that someone's trying to communicate with you. I believe that, um, it might have something to do with what's going on when you're awake. Your dreams can show . . . . like, what's bothering you, your fears, problems, sadness.

Speaker 3: I guess I did. Maybe I dreamed last night, but I don't know now.

I think dreams are an opening into the unconscious mind, I really do believe that, and, ah, I think that, uh, they can be of value, when, uh, interpreted in certain ways. But, I don't understand *my* dreams. But they must be important, they're part of your mind. They must be important in some way.

Listening 2: Dreams (Page 135)

Did you dream last night? What did you dream about? You might not remember your dreams, but people usually dream four to six times a night. Dreams can be short, only about ten minutes, but others can continue for an hour or more. People dream in color.

Men are more aggressive in their dreams, and they often fight or become angry at other men. Women often dream about friends and people they like. More than half of all dreams are unpleasant or frightening. The most common dream is that someone or something is chasing you. You are running and something is in back of you. Other common dreams are dreams of falling, losing your teeth, flying, or being in an accident.

What is the meaning of these dreams? Many psychologists think that dreams are "night work." They say that dreams help us look at our lives, our hopes, and our fears. They believe that in our dreams, we face problems and try to solve them. We look at our fears. We try out different personalities; at times we might be aggressive and talkative, but at other times we might be frightened and shy.

We often dream in symbols. Symbols are pictures that stand for or mean something else. Some psychologists think that these symbols might represent people or things in our lives. For example, a king and a queen might represent our parents. Small animals might stand for children. A long trip might mean we are worried about death or the death of someone in our family. If we are crossing a river, it might mean that we are at an important decision or time in our lives. But, if we get across the river in the dream, we believe we will be successful. If we do not make it across, we are afraid of failure.

We can have the same dream over and over. The dream may always be the same or it might have different endings. Our minds are working and playing, making movies about our lives.

Page 137

E. Finish the Sentence Listen to the first part of each sentence. Circle the second part of the sentence.

1. Some dreams are very long, . . .
2. Men's dreams are often aggressive, . . .
3. I know that I dreamed last night, . .
4. I remember my dreams when I first wake up, . . .
5. I often remember my dreams, ...
6. I sometimes dream about my father, . . .

Structure (Page 138)

B. Dictation Listen and write the sentences you hear.

1. You might see a terrible accident in your dream.
2. A king and queen might represent your parents.
3. Small animals might stand for children.
4. Someone you love might die.
5. You might take a trip in your dream.
6. You might have the same dream again and again.

Pronunciation (Page 138)

Pronunciation Note: Word stress

Stress can put special emphasis on any word or words in a sentence. Stress can change the meaning of the sentence.

I néver dream.

'I never dream.

A. Word Stress Listen carefully and mark the stressed word in each pair.

1. a. He <u>snores</u> all night.
   b. He snores <u>all</u> night.
2. a. You should go to bed <u>earlier</u>.
   b. You <u>should</u> go to bed earlier.
3. a. I want to hear about your <u>dream</u>.
   b. I want to hear about <u>your</u> dream.
4. a. What's the <u>meaning</u> of that dream?
   b. What's the meaning of <u>that</u> dream?
5. a. Dreams can be <u>frightening</u>.
   b. Dreams <u>can</u> be frightening.
6. a. I can't tell <u>her</u> my dream.
   b. I <u>can't</u> tell her my dream.
7. a. <u>I</u> never have nightmares.
   b. I <u>never</u> have nightmares.

Listening 3: Tell Me About Your Dream (Page 139)

Dream 1

I had a terrible dream last night. It was about my father. I saw him very clearly. He was on a ladder, very high, washing windows. It was the house where we used to live when I was a child. And I called, "Dad, be careful." Because he wasn't holding on. And he smiled and said, "Don't worry." Then he started to fall, very, very slowly. It seemed that he was falling for two or three minutes, in slow motion. And I tried to scream, but I couldn't. And he hit the ground.

Dream 2

I sometimes dream that I'm pregnant or that someone leaves a baby at our front door. You know, I already have three children and I don't want any more, so I don't know why I dream this.

Dream 3

When I was younger, I had, oh boy, these dreams, mostly about my parents, often about my mother. And I sometimes redream my dreams, I dream them again and again until I dream them right. And I remember this one dream especially.

My mother and her friends and I were leaving the supermarket. We were walking into the parking lot. And as we were getting in the car, this group of men came up and stood all around us. They were no good. Now, I tried to get everybody in the car, but I couldn't get everybody in the car. And I woke up and it was like, BOOM! Wrong! And I went back to sleep again and I redreamed it. This time, I got everybody in the car, and I closed the door, but the window was open. This man was able to get his hand in. I woke up and I said, "Uh-uh. Oh no." I went back to sleep again. And this last time in my dream, I got everybody in, got the door closed, the window closed, and drove off.

Dream 4

A few nights ago, I had a dream that something was chasing me. I don't remember how the dream began, but I was running. I was running through the woods. Well, it was more like a jungle, the trees and grass and bushes were really thick. I was running and screaming. Some kind of animal was behind me, I couldn't see it, but I heard it. It made a lot of noise, like a pig. Then my husband woke me up and said, "What's the matter? You're crying. It's all right. You're having a nightmare."

Dream 5

At times I dream about finding money. It's never a lot of money, it's always coins. I'm walking down the street. And I look on the sidewalk and I see a few quarters and dimes. I walk a little further, and there's another five or six quarters. Then I look ahead, and I see money, but just coins, everywhere, on the sidewalk and on the street and under the cars. I just pick them up and put 'em in my pockets.

Dream 6

I have a recurring dream about a river. I'm young, about 11 or 12. I'm playing by the river with my brother and sister. It's a big, wide river. And suddenly, in the middle, we see a young woman in the river. She's holding on to something, I think it's a piece of wood.

She's calling for help. There's no adult around and no boat and we don't know what to do. The river is moving fast, and she moves past us, still calling for help. And we just stand there and watch her going down the river.

Unit 14: Credit Cards

Listening 1: Person on the Street (Page 144)

Interview Question: Do you have a credit card?

Speaker 1: A credit card? I have seven or eight credit cards. Let's see – I have four or five credit cards from my favorite stores, and a gas credit card, and a bank credit card.

Speaker 2: No. I pay cash for everything. And I pay my bills by check. I don't want a credit card.

Speaker 3: Yes, but just one. You have to have a credit card when you travel. You need one to make hotel reservations or to rent a car.

Speaker 4: Yeah. I only have two. I use the Internet a lot. You can't order anything if you don't have a credit card.

Listening 2: Radio Talk Show (Page 146)

Part 1: Understanding the Problem

ANNOUNCER: And now to the call in session of our talk show. Jack Angeles, is manager of Volo Credit Cards. Jack, we have several people waiting on the line. Now, to our first caller. This is Mike. Mike is from Arizona.

JACK: Hi Mike.

MIKE: Hi Jack. Thanks for taking my call . . . Jack, I bought a big flat screen TV last year. I paid $5,000 for the TV and put it on my credit card. Every month when my bill comes, I pay $100, but my principal only goes down a few dollars. I've been paying my card for a year, but I still owe almost $4,800. What's going on here?

JACK: Mike, do you know what your interest rate is?

MIKE: I think it's 22%.

JACK: OK, you are only paying the minimum amount on your card every month. When you make a payment, most of your money is going for the interest. It's going to take you more than ten years to pay for that TV.

Listening 2: Radio Talk Show (Page 146)

Part 2: Understanding Interest Rates

JACK: It's going to take you more than ten years to pay for that TV.

MIKE: Ten years!

JACK: Mike, check the interest rate on your bill again.

MIKE: I have the bill right here. Yes, that's it . . . 22%.

JACK: OK, you are only paying the minimum amount on your card every month. When you make a payment, most of your money is going for the interest. Mike, if you continue to pay only $100 a month, it will take you almost 11 years pay off your card, and, you'll pay about $8,700 in interest! So your TV will really cost you $13,700. If you pay $200 a month, you will need about three years to pay off your card, and your interest will be about $1,750. That means your TV will cost you $6,750. That's still a lot of money! Try to pay off $300 a month. You will be able to pay off your credit card in less than two years, let's see, yes, in 21 months. And your interest will only be about $1,020. If you can pay $300 a month, the total cost of your TV will be $6,020. But, be careful and don't buy anything else with your credit card.

Pronunciation (Page 148)

Pronunciation Note: More Practice with Linking
Linking means joining or saying together. Link the final consonant of a word with the beginning vowel in the next word.
rent a car
two and a half years
I bought a computer.
I have a credit card.

A. Linking Listen and repeat these short phrases and sentences.

1. rent a car
2. a year and a half
3. make a payment
4. pay off
5. It's a call in show.
6. Mike is from Arizona.
7. You need a credit card to make a reservation.
8. You'll need about two years to pay off your card.

Listening 3: Credit Card Problems (Page 149)

A: I had a credit card. But now I don't. The credit card company took it away.

B: They took it away?

A: And it wasn't my fault.

B: I don't know what you mean.

A: I had a credit card. And I was good about not charging too much and paying it off every month. Then, last year, my sister wanted to use my card.

B: Uh-oh!

A: I didn't want to give it to her, but she needed to buy airline tickets to go on vacation and she didn't have the money. She promised to pay off the card.

B: How much did she charge?

A: Two thousand dollars.

B: Two thousand dollars?

A: When the first bill came, I gave it to her, but she didn't pay it. When the next bill came, there was a late fee and a finance charge. I didn't have the money to pay it. I gave the bill to my sister and told her she had to pay the bill, but she couldn't. The bill kept going up and I couldn't pay it. The company called me and called me.

B: What finally happened?

A: They took away my credit card and now I have bad credit and I can't get a car loan.

B: That's too bad.

INDEX

PHOTO CREDITS